The Skies I'm Under

*The rain and shine of parenting a child with
complex disabilities*

By Rachel Wright

*"Some moments are nice,
some are nicer,
some are even worth writing about."*
Charles Bukowski

1

First published in Great Britain by
Born at the Right Time Publishing

ISBN 978-0-9934915-0-4 (Paperback)
ISBN 978-0-9934915-1-1 (eBook-Mobi)
ISBN 978-0-9934915-2-8 (eBook-ePub)

Cover photo by Tim Wright 2007
Cover design by Ian Hutchins 2015
www.hutchinscreative.co.uk
Printed in England by 4edge 2015
www.4edge.co.uk

For Mum,
who has shown me motherhood never ends.

Prologue		5
	Part 1 In the beginning	
Chapter 1	Birth	10
Chapter 2	Name	19
Chapter 3	First Night	24
Chapter 4	Hope	33
Chapter 5	Home	39
Chapter 6	Truth	44
	Part 2 A New Normal	
Chapter 7	A New Year	54
Chapter 8	Community, God and Healing	59
Chapter 9	A Parable	66
Chapter 10	Tim's Story: First Day	69
Chapter 11	Running and Praying	75
Chapter 12	Words	79
Chapter 13	It's Not the Same	86
Chapter 14	Tim's Story: Doctor v Dad	93
Chapter 15	Seizures	101
Chapter 16	Feeding	110
Chapter 17	Birthdays	115
Chapter 18	Not Feeding	122
Chapter 19	I Get Knocked Down	128
Chapter 20	Take 2	135
Chapter 21	Jonah	143
Chapter 22	Tim's Story: France	149
	Part 3 Learning To Live Again	
Chapter 23	Acceptance	158
Chapter 24	School	163
Chapter 25	Marathon	170
Chapter 26	A Trip to the Library	175
Chapter 27	Travelling Without Baggage	180
Chapter 28	Working and Weeping	185
Chapter 29	Funerals	191
Chapter 30	Another View	196
Epilogue	December 2014	199
Glossary		202

Prologue

*"You know you're in love when you can't fall asleep
because reality is finally better than your dreams."*

Dr. Seuss

Traces of sunlight creep round the curtains as night fades and echoes of unfamiliar footsteps grow in the corridor. The door creaks and my eyes open to see my young son. I tremble as he walks towards me with his short, thick brown hair and familiar smile. His arms reach out for an embrace and I look into his deep blue eyes, while a smile monopolises my face.

We connect.

I see him and he sees me.

His lips form the word 'Mummy' but the message becomes distorted like an out of tune radio.

I wake and my ears focus in on the baby monitor spewing out whines from another room. Groggily I get up to help my son, as the thin veil of sleep reveals the chasm between my dreams and reality.

Approaching his bed I lean in and whisper, "Come on, let me turn you over so you can go back to sleep."

Lifting limp legs I turn my son to face me. Manipulating his body, I secure him between padded supports and pillows, and then I wait.

My face rests by his ear and my hand soothes his shoulder while he arches and moans. I know it's going to take time to settle him and my cold feet long for warmth, so I slide under the duvet. His excited giggles demonstrate approval as our frames entwine and relax.

"Come on, let's go to sleep now," I hush.

Consciousness fades and my dream world descends once more.

"Good morning. Did you have a snuggle with me in bed last night?" I ask.

"Mummy, you got into *my* bed. My hip was sore. Moving me helped."

"Oh and I thought you just wanted a cuddle."

"I like cuddles… What day is it?"

"Monday."

"Is it assembly?"

"I'm not sure. Why?"

"I don't like it."

"You don't like assembly? Why, because it scares you?"

"Yes."

"What's scary? Is it the clapping, the singing, the people?"

"I don't like it all."

"The world is scary and confusing but you can trust me. Even when life doesn't make sense, I will try to protect you as best I can."

My little boy's furrowed brow indicates thinking.

"Don't you believe me?" I ask. "I love you. I won't leave you. Even when you don't understand what is happening I can see things you can't."

"I get scared and want to listen to my music."

"I know, but it isn't good to always listen to music."

"I like music. It makes me feel safe."

"It might make you feel safe but the people who love you

keep you safe. You can't always have your music."

"Why?"

"Listening to your music means you miss out on things."

"But music makes me happy. Nothing else is good."

"That's not true. You are good. You are my wonderful little boy. You are unique and you make this world… you make my world a better place."

"What?"

"You do. The things you can't do aren't as important as I once thought."

Another quizzical look is directed straight into my eyes. I kiss his soft round cheek and whisper so close I can feel warm breath on my face.

"You are created. You love, have relationships and make people smile. I'm sorry it is hard and scary. I wish I could make it better. I wish I understood."

I hold my son tight and feel overwhelmed with love.

"The truth is, even with all you can't do, you shine. You change people and you have changed me. I don't understand it and it scares me but I'm trying to trust God, the way I'm asking you to trust me."

"Mummy?"

"Yes?"

"You need to wake up."

"Why?"

"I need the toilet and the only reason we are talking like this is because you are dreaming again."

"Really? Just a couple more minutes, please. I love talking like this."

I wake once again to see the creased and handsome face of my son as he begins to groan.

"Good morning. Did you have a sneaky Mummy-cuddle in bed last night?"

"Bu bu," comes the reply, as a grin streaks across his face.

"Ok, do you need a wee? I'll get you the toilet."

"Mmm bu," he responds.

I lumber out of bed, my feet slapping on the cold hard wood floor. I lift my son's pained, stiff body and strap him securely onto the commode. Haphazardly he raises his head.

I react with a kiss and stroke his hair.

"Good morning my lovely boy."

Moments later my son's lips kiss the air in return as his whole body laughs in pleasure.

"I love you too." I smile. "Let me get your medications and I will tell you about today."

Part 1
In the Beginning

1

Birth: 12th October 2005

"A life can get knocked into a new orbit by a car crash, a lottery win or just a bleary-eyed consultant giving bad news in a calm voice."
David Mitchell

In the autumn of 2005, I woke in the middle of the night with a niggling sense of uncertainty. Unable to settle I slunk out of bed so as not to disturb my husband, Tim, and sat in the dark, newly decorated nursery. The faint orange streetlight illuminated our box room as I sat in silence. Surrounded by the aroma of freshly painted walls and sense of new, I felt cocooned by the stillness of the midnight hour.

The cot opposite was ready and waiting, with a brand new mobile dangling pale-coloured jungle creatures overhead. My hospital bag lay packed on freshly laid laminate flooring, while a pine chest of drawers sat filled with sleep suits and socks that looked impossibly small.

Excitement had grown over recent weeks but a seed of fear now began to swell. I couldn't feel my baby move. I tried to quash what I thought were the emotional, neurotic feelings of a hormonal, pregnant woman. Yet all I had recently seen in Uganda reminded me that a healthy baby does not necessarily follow pregnancy.

For the past year I had worked as a nurse in Uganda and then New Zealand while Tim practiced medicine alongside me. We spent the year testing out the possibility of our dream to live long-term in a developing country. The image of a young mum coming to the homely clinic in the city's Namuwongo district of Kampala was fresh in my mind.

Wearing a long floral skirt and loose top, she arrived one bright morning and sat beside a friend in the neat reception area holding a bundle of baby blankets. The clinic was otherwise quiet, except for the humdrum of the street outside, and Tim immediately called the pair into the small consultation room. I sat in to observe and assist if necessary.

Her friend took control and placed a swaddled newborn girl on the treatment couch in the corner of the room. The mum tentatively sat on a chair opposite while her friend spoke of how the young woman had delivered her baby earlier in the day. They were concerned the baby was sick.

Tim examined the fragile creature. Sombrely he raised his stethoscope to his ears and placed it tenderly on the baby's chest. Moments passed slowly before he lifted his head and began to speak in low, soft tones. He explained the baby girl wasn't sick but had died. The muggy African heat felt suddenly oppressive as I involuntarily inhaled a sharp intake of breath. The stunned look on the young woman's face was permanently imprinted in my mind. She sagged under the weight of the news as grief swamped her slight frame.

Unceremoniously the friend lifted the baby's limp body, carried it back across the reception area and out the door. The young mum nodded her head in gratitude, and gingerly shuffled outside. Grief stricken, she followed her dead baby into the dusty Kampala streets.

11

My mind reeled with memories as I held my silent belly and gazed at the shadows our baby's mobile etched on the yellow wall behind the cot. Tears began to fall as I remembered my university days. My housemate Nneka had lived through the grief of losing her younger sister and in the months after she played the song *Kiss the son* by Kevin Prosch over and over again. I recalled its lyrics of praise amidst heartbreak, brokenness and pain.

Within the vacuum of the night the song reverberated in my head. Like a mantra I replayed the refrain:

'Though you slay me I will trust you Lord.'

I choked out the words, as tears tripped my lips and an internal battle raged.

Was there something wrong with my baby?

Was I being irrational?

I decided my fear was greater than the facts as I had felt my baby throughout the previous day. After an unknown amount of time, I gathered my emotions and returned to bed. Climbing under the covers I allowed my cold feet to surreptitiously wake Tim.

"What's the matter?" My husband's arm came across and held my bulging waist.

"I'm worried the baby isn't moving."

"What time is it?"

"Just after two."

"It was only a few hours ago you were complaining your hot chocolate was being kicked off your bump."

"Yeh, you're right."

Reassuringly the image of us both relaxing on our friends', Rachel and Russell's, sofa sprang to life. We had spent the evening helping them strip wallpaper in preparation for their second son's arrival. As reward for our labour we were provided

12

with refreshments and while I rested my hot chocolate on my bump my baby had kicked.

We agreed that I would contact the maternity unit first thing in the morning if nothing had changed. I lay still and enjoyed Tim's arm resting on me. Having met at a Christian youth camp as kids we had already enjoyed nearly ten years as a couple. We had grown up together and shared the same sense of adventure. Even our chosen careers confirmed we just seemed to fit. Effortlessly I drifted off to sleep.

The next morning I woke and showered immediately, the feelings of concern having dissipated with the night.

"Have you felt any movements?" asked Tim, from round the bathroom door.

"I don't think so," I confirmed.

"Call the midwife as soon as you've showered. I've got to rush, I'm late for work."

A quick kiss and I was home alone.

When I phoned the midwife she used the same steady tone as Tim and suggested I had some breakfast before making my way to the antenatal ward. I called my closest friend, Rachel, and persuaded her to take me to the hospital instead of our planned swim. She picked me up and rather than bringing my hospital bag, I carried my swimming costume. It was now my chosen form of exercise since I stopped being able to run. I expected to be seen and reassured quickly, with time to spare for a quick dip.

On the ward I walked straight to the desk,

"Hi, I called earlier because I can't feel my baby move."

"What's your name?" asked the midwife.

"Rachel Wright."

The young woman glanced at the large black book in front of her.

"Oh yes, you spoke to me. Come right this way."

I was shown into a bay with six beds where I perched myself on top of starched white sheets while I was strapped to a monitor. Immediately hearing and seeing my baby's heartbeat pacified me. I sighed with relief while my own heart rate slowed.

The midwives, however, seemed concerned that the monitor was displaying a 'sleeping trace', so I was left connected, with a small red button to press if I felt any movement. Tim rushed up from the elderly care ward where he was working and, on hearing the heartbeat, hurried back to work reassured.

By late morning I was sent for an ultrasound scan. I didn't want to know the sex of our baby before Tim, so I didn't watch the screen. I was comforted, though, by the sonographer saying the blood flow around my baby's brain, body and umbilical cord were good. No amount of prodding and poking, however, would make my baby wake up. I headed back to the antenatal ward, scan results in hand, and was told to wait.

Rachel went to collect her son from nursery and I was left with my thoughts, whilst discreetly watching those around me. Across the bay I saw Julia, a woman from my antenatal class, also strapped to a machine with an anxious face and concerned partner holding her hand.

I lay back and tried to rest. My head hit the cold metal bar of the NHS bed frame as I closed my eyes and remembered how I got here.

Eight months earlier I had popped into the supermarket on the way home from work and bought a pregnancy test. Having played my part I left it in the bathroom of our hospital accommodation for Tim to read. He came into the living room

14

and immediately I saw the smile on his face; we were going to have a baby. We hugged, while he doggedly held on to the piece of plastic I had just peed on.

Although I lived well with my pregnancy I was disappointed I didn't evolve into an 'earth mother'. I felt as though an alien in my stomach was transforming me, rather than me fulfilling my cosmic role as a woman. The whole thing felt weird, while the nausea and vomiting made me feel really rough.

At thirty-eight weeks pregnant I had finished work expectant that I would soon experience the 'nesting' everyone had promised. No scrubbing or motherly homemaking occurred. My only relationship with baking had happened when I tried to impress my new husband by steaming his favourite treacle sponge pudding, but that didn't last long. It seemed even my impending baby didn't spark my baking gene to ignite.

"Any movements?" The midwife's voice woke me from my daydreaming.

"No, afraid not." She stretched out the foetal readings in her hand and squiggled her name.

"Hmm… still a sleeping trace." Like a four-letter word, the explanation was now spat from her lips.

"The doctor will be with you in a minute."

After a short consultation the doctor made it clear she wanted to deliver me, either by caesarean or induction. An examination showed I was a centimetre dilated, although I hadn't experienced any contractions.

A shortage of beds delayed my transfer. So I called my mum and dad in Buckingham to tell them their next grandchild would arrive soon. The strong relationship I have with my parents meant I instantly picked up the panic in my mum's voice. I tried to reassure her, asserting there was no need to rush. So they jumped in the car and headed straight for Southend-on-sea.

I called Tim on my mobile via the hospital switchboard, and once he arrived we were shown to a more sterile room on the labour ward. There I clambered into a clinical gown and my waters were broken. Surrounded by monitors and equipment we discussed the prospect of a caesarean.

"The good news is there is no meconium in your waters suggesting your baby hasn't been distressed in any way," the doctor chirped.

"Great." I nodded.

"I'm ninety percent sure your baby is fine but being that you are a first time mum it would take too long to induce you. It's not ideal but I think we should prepare you for theatre and a caesarean."

I looked at Tim and we had a silent conversation with our eyes.

"Ok," said Tim, taking the words from my mouth. "It's not what we planned but we don't want to take any risks."

"The most important thing is to get your baby out fit and well," the doctor urged, and we both smiled in agreement.

"So what happens now?"

The following minutes remained calm and jovial as everything started happening very quickly. An anaesthetist arrived and poked around my spine to insert a very big needle. Before long, my legs were lifted onto the trolley fizzing and tingling, as if they no longer belonged to me.

In theatre, Tim sat by my head as we chatted and joked about nothing important. He averted his eyes from all that was happening behind the curtain erected to separate us from the lower part of my body. Apparently cutting people open is fine until it's your wife, then it becomes distinctly less acceptable.

The hustle and bustle of theatre continued around us. The chatter of the obstetrician and midwives was accompanied by the clatter of instruments and trolleys. Everything remained fairly un-rushed and lighthearted. Before long the operation began and I was cut open.

*

Just after 2pm on Wednesday 12th October 2005 a slimy, limp baby was removed from my womb with the exclamation from the delivering doctor that we had a boy. Tim and I smiled at each other.

"A boy!" we exclaimed in unison. Within a few moments, however, I became concerned that I couldn't hear my son cry and I sent Tim to investigate.

As he took the long slow steps back across the theatre he considered his words and gently lowered his head next to mine.

"What's wrong? What going on?" I implored.

"He isn't breathing." Tim's gaze penetrated my heart. "The doctors are trying to resuscitate him now." A kiss on my forehead sealed his words.

"Go back and watch over him. Then tell me what's happening."

Suddenly my mind and spirit were as numb and disjointed as my legs.

Tim retraced his steps, passing familiar equipment and suddenly sullen faces. The anaesthetist behind me touched my shoulder and I sobbed. Although I was unable to feel most of my body the pain was overwhelming.

Medical staff started buzzing around and after several

minutes of Tim going backwards and forwards I got a glimpse of the top of my son's head. I was encouraged to give it a quick kiss as my faceless baby was whisked off to the neonatal intensive care unit to be ventilated.

Then the sobbing really began, interrupting the uncomfortable hush that engulfed the theatre. The flood of my tears hit like a tsunami and in an instant the landscape of my world became unrecognisable.

2

Name

"Names have power."

Rick Riordan

As I lay in recovery, I had no idea the extent to which my world had changed. Listening to the bleeps of the monitors and footsteps of people passing the bottom of my bed, I drifted in and out of a morphine-induced sleep.

In my memory I lay alone for quite a while. Tim was visiting our son, calling our parents or changing out of his theatre blues. The environment was so familiar but the experience foreign. I knew the components of my surroundings; the smell of the bleach, starchy sheets and glaring lights. I have cared for patients recovering from operations but the perspective of looking out from my bed as the patient, was a stark role reversal. As I lay in eerie silence I realised not only was my perspective different but that my expectations were unravelling.

Tim returned and stood with me, sharing snippets of information he had gleaned from medical staff. Once I was awake, and sufficiently over my anaesthetic, I was wheeled to the postnatal ward on my bed via neonatal intensive care.

The large cumbersome trolley careered into the tiny intensive care bay where our baby was the only patient. I held my breath in anticipation; my life was distilled into this

19

moment. I couldn't see my future and suddenly so much of my past seemed irrelevant. I looked around and took in the scene.

Staff walked about whispering, connecting lines and reading monitors. The subdued light cast soft shadows while a controlled calm hung thick in the air. I had found pregnancy alien and obscure, and now the same feelings were continuing into my next phase of motherhood. As my bed drew up next to a tiny plastic box, I knew I was approaching a little person that I deeply loved and yet didn't know. My head and heart felt disjointed. I was going to see my baby's face for the first time.

Tentatively I sat more upright in order to get a better view because his appearance wasn't easy to distinguish in the dim light. A tube connected to a ventilator jolted out of his mouth, while a thin nasogastric tube snaked across his cheek. His dark hair though, was clear to see. A defined ring of fine black hair marked out the edges of an old man's bald patch.

My first thought took me by surprise; he looked ridiculous. I know I am supposed to say how consumed I was with love or maternal emotion but in truth my only thought was that he appeared to be a complete hypochondriac. Tim has always been very cynical about the beauty of a newborn baby and this swollen, puffy eyed newborn was not helping my counter argument. His resemblance to a balding Cabbage Patch Kid was uncanny.

As I took my first glance at my son's face my parents and our minister rushed in the door with a sense of urgency and panic. Through tears and broken words they prayed for our little boy, desperately hoping for a miracle and speedy recovery.

The news from the medical staff, however, remained bleak. He needed ventilation to breathe and so far there was little indication as to exactly what was going on, why this had happened or how bad things were. My hospital bed took up practically all of the floor space in intensive care so I couldn't stay long and after a short while we left our son in the hands of the doctors.

As I was wheeled to the postnatal ward my maternal instinct tugged at my heart. Seeing my son through the casing of an incubator, my fingers having not yet touched his skin, was not nature's way.

I was pushed into my plain but brightly coloured hospital side room with tired paintwork and an uncomfortable comfy chair. My parents left us and we quickly decided we needed to name our son. Baby Wright didn't give him the dignity he deserved.

The previous year in Uganda our understanding of the importance of names had deepened. Our friends there were given incredibly descriptive, meaningful names. Some were named after the day they were born, such as Wednesday, while others were given more thoughtful names such as Beauty or Precious. Our friend Okut got his name from the weather, because it was raining the morning of his birth. Although there were rare occasions when parents used names to curse their children, most gave loving and thoughtful names such as Grace, Joy or Hope. We had grown to believe a name is powerful and wanted the name we gave our son to have a meaning beyond it sounding good with Wright.

We had thought about names but decided to wait until we met our baby before making a choice. I liked the idea of our son having a family name; it certainly saved us the effort of being original. The bald head and dark hair triggered thoughts of my dad.

My dad is incredible, an opinion I share with Tim. He is a remarkable, Godly man full of humility and grace. He has a soft

21

Irish accent nurtured on the streets of Belfast and his name is...
Norman. Now, I don't want to be namist (if there is such a
word) or cause offence, but Norman was never going to happen.
Norman cultivates images of a man with a goofy smile and flat
cap, not a little boy fighting for his life in intensive care.

My dad's middle name, however, is Samuel after his
father. Grandad Sammy died when my dad was only seventeen,
yet Grandma Hessie had so lovingly spoken about her husband
that her tales and memories filled my head as though they were
my own. When we discovered Samuel means 'God hears' we
decided that it would suit just fine. We really needed our prayers
to be heard.

Having chosen a family name, his middle name was easy.
Tim's wonderful dad and maternal grandad are called David; so
two names satisfied two generations on both sides of our family.
Perfect.

By tea time we had sent a group text to all our friends
asking for prayers for our little boy, Samuel David Wright. We
sat huddled together, sorrowful and uncertain while our message
broke into our friends' days. Their routine patterns of life
continued while cataclysmic changes were being experienced in
our world.

Once I had gathered my strength Tim helped me into the
bathroom where I took off my theatre gown and pulled on a T-
shirt and tracksuit trousers. Steadying myself on the sink rim I
turned on the tap to wash my face.

As the water gushed around the bowl I stared at the ripples
glistening in the artificial light. Raising my head, I caught the
reflection of my hazel eyes staring back at me. My long brown
hair sat limp on my shoulders, my pale face amplifying my
freckles. Life so far had felt so unexceptional. The image I saw
betrayed the change I felt inside, as the same simple and

predictable Rachel appeared to gaze back.

I splashed cold water on my face and was wiping it dry when a knock at the door indicated a wheelchair had been located. It was time to go and visit my son, Sammy.

3

First Night

*"Even when the way goes through Death Valley,
I'm not afraid when you walk at my side."*

Psalm 23v4

Flanked by my parents, we visited Sammy only to find there were no signs of improvement and the news remained grim. He needed help with all of his essential functions and sported small bruises on all four limbs; evidence of several failed attempts to insert catheters into his veins.

Tim strained to push my wheelchair next to his incubator, suggesting he was wheeling a weight greater than my post pregnancy body. I noticed my son wore a nappy; one I hadn't put on. His tiny body lay encased in a clear plastic box, littered with instruments and leads. As I gazed, I tried to allow the machinery to melt away, letting my eyes focus on Sammy. Standing next to our baby we were engulfed by a deafening silence, absent of an infant crying.

We were instructed that we could touch our son once we had washed our hands. Like a practiced professional I turned on the tap and dispensed the slimy liquid soap. As the lather developed its scent hit my nose and etched this moment in time permanently upon my memory. For years to come the same fragrance would trigger a flashback to this juncture in my life. Then, once my hands were dried, I hobbled over to the incubator. Like a teasing tactile game of discovery, I inserted my hands through the little portholes, allowing my fingers to seek out my son.

I stood sore and bewildered. The surrounding machines revealed information my head understood but my heart did not, and I clung to Tim for support. We had grown from a couple to a family. We mumbled and purred any words we could find and laid them before our son. My parents took photos of our tear stained faces, hugging the incubator that encased Sammy.

Time passed and I grew tired, unable to stand or sit next to our son. My parents went back to our house and we returned to the postnatal ward. Over dinner we half-heartedly watched England beat Poland on the TV. While across the corridor medical staff worked towards saving our son's life, we temporarily sat in a parallel universe where eating food and watching football was normal.

As night descended the nurses on the postnatal ward broke the rules and allowed Tim to stay. When all the other fathers were sent home, Tim and I held each other rather than a baby. We were given a zed bed, that wasn't used, and eventually I fell asleep in the arms of my husband. Then, throughout the night I kept waking with a jolt. Panicked and afraid, the realisation of what had happened dawned on me afresh. With hushed voices Tim and I crept out of bed, and I hustled back into my wheelchair. Each time we arrived on the neonatal unit, medical staff beavered around, apparently unaware of the time.

With each journey, the short distance from our side room to the ward grew longer, as each visit brought more bad news. By the time we woke for a third time we were beginning to doubt whether we really wanted to go back. On arrival we found Sammy having an urgent ultrasound of his brain because of more complications.

When light finally seeped into our side room on Thursday morning we woke glad that our son had survived the night.

"Good morning," came the familiar voice of our friend Carol as she peeked around the door. Without permission my eyes welled and I began to weep as she approached and hugged me.

"Pack your stuff. I've arranged another room for you."

Carol helped collect our things and I was wheeled towards the labour ward, where she worked as a senior midwife. She ushered us out of the sterile hospital corridor into a large tranquil room called the Butterfly Suite. Pictures hung on the walls as a floral duvet straddled a pine double bed.

Soon breakfast in the Butterfly Suite arrived. I poured milk into the shallow white hospital bowl containing my cornflakes and instinctively began to say grace. Throughout my childhood I had been taught the importance of being grateful, in particular saying thank you for my food. As words gathered in my mouth, only a few passed my lips.

"Heavenly Father, thank…" I choked. Raising my head, I looked into the heaviness of Tim's dark green eyes and unshaven face. In his gaze I caught a reflection of my own pain and questions.

"Thanks for our food," was all I could muster before silence fell, only to be interrupted by my muffled sobs and the crowing seagulls outside.

After breakfast we washed and got dressed, ready for the ward round. We were shown into a small room on the neonatal ward and asked to wait. As we stepped in I recognised all the traits of a room tailored to break bad news. The small two-seater sofa, single chair and box of tissues spoke volumes. When Sam's doctor arrived he asked us questions relating to what had happened before Sam's birth and then he explained what had happened since. He knew Tim was a doctor and I a nurse, so he spoke using medical terminology, explaining things with clarity and depth. He answered all our questions but was unable to reassure us.

He explained that the next forty-eight hours were crucial, as Sam was still at risk of dying. We were given hope of a slim chance he could escape this episode without future consequences, although it was much more likely that he would suffer long-term side effects. There was also a slim chance he would suffer severe brain damage that would have a dramatic and complex impact on his future. Sammy was diagnosed with grade 2/3 Hypoxic Ischaemic Encephalopathy. We took in as much information as we could; ready to face an unpredictable day.

As morning became afternoon our relatives began to visit. Between us, Tim and I have six brothers and three sisters, so there were a lot of people who wanted to meet the new addition to the family. My eldest brother, Paul, and his eight-month pregnant wife, Claire, were the first past our door. Paul stepped into the room and caught my eye.

"Oh Rachel, I'm so sorry," was all he said, before he broke down in tears. Sometimes, just showing up and crying is more precious than any well-chosen words.

Hugs and tears continued through the day as we introduced our family to Sammy. My mother-in-law, Janine, visited while my father-in-law, David, was on the other side of the Atlantic on a business trip. It was a really tough time for him, feeling so helpless and far from home.

Later that afternoon, Carol visited again gently suggesting

I try to express some milk. Sam had a nasogastric tube going up his nose and into his stomach. When he was well enough, he would be fed through this tube. I decided if that time ever came, I wanted him to be given breast milk.

I was taken aback when the machine brought into my room to extract milk from my breasts was the size of a car battery and resembled an instrument of torture. It had no fine design, no exciting features, no comfort mode and no manual. The surreal experience of sitting alone, propped up on a bed with a small megaphone attached to my breast, while a noisy machine sucked and whirred, was by far, my weirdest to date. It reminded me of the Alanis Morissette song *Ironic*. I remember listening to it with Tim as we drove around the country lanes of Sussex in the summer of 1995 when we first started dating. But instead of 'It's like rain on your wedding day...' the breast pump's swirling added an instrumental backing to my own lyrics:

'It's like a breast pump to extract some milk
For your baby son, who might not survive.'

Admittedly it's less catchy, but you get the gist. For me the significance of producing milk that may become futile, trumped a damp wedding dress. The chorus of that song is spot on though:

'Life has a funny way of sneaking up on you when you think everything's okay.'

So, I lay on my bed and pretended I was Daisy the cow. I didn't feel as though there was anything natural or motherly about what I was doing. When I later repeated this painful process, Carol had returned with a Polaroid photo of Sammy in his incubator, to help with milk production. I'm not sure how

28

this thoughtful gesture affected lactation but it certainly increased the production of tears.

Eventually, I strode into the neonatal ward and placed a small bottle of colostrum on top of Sam's incubator. My sense of achievement was huge. This was something I could do; something that only I could do. At a time when I couldn't hold my son, this was a physical expression of me being a mum. So, I took to making milk as though it was a mission sent from God. After a few days my nipples were sore and blistered with the pressure of the machine. Each time I started expressing, I would grip Tim's hand, bite my tongue and allow stinging, silent tears to fall down my cheeks in pain. Then, nearly a week after I started using the blasted pump, someone showed me a little knob on the top right-hand corner that, when turned anti-clockwise, reduced the suction strength. It had been on full pelt from the beginning. If only there had been a manual.

Time continued with a momentum of its own. Between expressing, eating, resting and greeting visitors, time passed effortlessly. I felt as though we were exercising the habits of living, in slow motion. We silently stood bewildered in the eye of a storm, as we watched others beaver frantically around us. Family came and went, medical staff cared for Sam and my parents were an ever-loving presence.

When Carol encouraged me to express milk, my mum gave invaluable reassurance and practical support. She ensured I had the necessary drinks, treats and kind words to make emotional tasks more bearable. She shielded us from the need to repeatedly explain things and shopped for anything we may need, including some things we didn't. Then, when my grief was too great she held me.

Even though we were surrounded by people who loved us,

I felt alone. I recall a time, during our travelling the year before, when we became lost running around a lake in the South Island of New Zealand. We had parked the car alongside a walking track, tied-up our trainers and headed off for a late afternoon jog. Winter sun glinted through the trees as we raced between the vibrant green woodland soaking up the foreign sounds and sights. After a while of our feet crunching across the decaying undergrowth, the well-marked path we had been following suddenly disappeared. We had managed to veer off course and become lost. Tim portrayed the epitome of calm while I jittered with anxiety and dread, my fear of the dark magnifying my emotions. After a very long twenty minutes we eventually found our way again and the rest of our run was filled with relief.

On the second night of Sam's life we lay together on the Butterfly Suite's double bed and felt alone. Isolation similar to what we had experienced on our run near Mount Ruapehu had returned. We had left the path walked by everyone else and found ourselves in unexplored and unfamiliar territory. We didn't know if we would ever find our way again. Sammy remained on a ventilator, as darkness shrouded our whispers. We had been told the next twelve hours were critical, as Sam's life hung in the balance. Curled up in each other's arms, we talked quietly and timidly about the reality of our son dying, and the possibility of raising a disabled child.

We had witnessed and experienced loss but couldn't conceive the pain of losing Sammy. The turmoil of leaving the hospital without him, going back to a nursery without a baby to fill the cot, and planning a funeral were unfathomable. However, in that time and in that moment, we were brave enough to be brutally honest. When we dared to imagine the unthinkable and utter the incomprehensible we shocked ourselves by concluding that life might be harder than death.

30

We confessed to understanding the world of loss more than the world of disability. We could imagine our hearts breaking, being forever changed by grief, then piecing our lives back together. Grieving and moving on, living after death, was conceivable but we couldn't see our future with a disabled son. We couldn't envisage the on-going sorrow of parenting a child with a complex medical condition and unknown future.

If Sam died the practical routine of our lives would remain the same. I would eventually go back to work, as a nurse, and Tim would continue to train as a GP. We would live in our home and hopefully one day try and have another baby. The grief was incomprehensible but the rhythm of living would be familiar. Our sense of loss would be centred on a beautiful little boy we never really knew. We would grieve a dream, a hope and an expectation of what our family would have become.

As we tried to imagine our lives with Sammy living with a profound disability, neither the emotional nor the practical components of our world were familiar. It was difficult to picture life with the perpetual grief of our son not being able to do and be all we had hoped. How could we live without sharing with him our love for running, cycling and everything outdoors? We struggled to see our future with disability as well as losing our dream of living in a developing country. More simply, we didn't know what living with a disability was like and we didn't want to.

The unknowns were immense and suffocating. As we spoke of the cold harsh reality, ignoring the emotional grief of death, we decided our life might be less complicated if Sam's life ended. Every cell in our bodies wanted Sam to live and we would love and value him no less if he was disabled. Yet, in our darkest moment, we believed life without Sam might be easier than the transformation, pain and sacrifices needed, when loving and raising a severely disabled child.

As we lay in silence our words hung around us like shards of broken dreams suspended in the air. It wasn't a neat, tidy conversation that resulted in resolution. We opened the wounds of our fears and left them exposed to the air, each other and our God. No prayers were heard and neither peace, nor hope penetrated our sorrow and uncertainty. Yet in my husband's arms, in our honesty, brokenness and unity, I felt something greater. Something, or someone, bigger than the two people lying in the darkness filled the room and my heart. We weren't alone.

4

Hope

"Two roads diverged in a wood and I - I took the one less travelled"
Robert Frost

We continued to wake and visit Sam through that second night, walking through the labour ward as it echoed with the sound of mothers giving birth to screaming, healthy babies. I longed to hear Sam cry, see him move; hold his little body in my arms.

Gratefully, we greeted the light of Friday morning without any more bad news. Sam stabilised and his survival was less in doubt but the questions of disability hung thick in the air. We left the conversation from the night before securely sealed in the past and longed for recovery. On the third day of Sam's life, I finally held my son.

As I sat on a hard plastic chair beside his incubator, the military operation to manoeuvre all of the tubes and leads began. Amidst ringing monitors, Sam was gently laid into my arms. Tim knelt by my side and embraced us both. The machines faded as the son I held came into clear focus. This was my precious boy. I was a mother. Silent tears tickled my face as I kissed my son's head and held his fragile body.

"Hello my beautiful boy," I hushed, "Mummy and Daddy are here."

33

"Hi, Sammy. We love you very much." Tim kissed our son's forehead and raised his hand to stroke his brow. Looking into my husband's tired eyes I saw the determination of a father longing to protect his family.

In the dimly lit intensive care unit our first family photo shows exhausted faces; weary, worn, and smiling. Experiencing the warmth of Sam's body against my own felt as though a window had been thrown open. We dared to invite in much needed light and a glimmer of hope.

Over the following days, I grew in strength and spent increasingly more time by Sammy's incubator.

"Can I do that please?" I enquired.

As familiarity with the nursing staff grew, I dared to carry out Sam's care. My inexperience as a mother meant I had no idea how I should feel or behave but I knew how to be a nurse. Without thinking, I became increasingly comfortable with caring and naturally slipped into a familiar role and environment.

Perched on high stools we peered into Sam's incubator. Whilst chatting to the nurses we witnessed Sam's ventilator being removed, revealing his face. Sam, however, decided breathing wasn't important. Like a teenage boy from Essex, he simply shrugged his shoulders exclaiming, "Whatever!. Breavin?... Not that fussed, me! Take it or leave it."

The oxygen monitor strapped securely to his foot protested loudly while our own breaths faltered. Numbers flashed red and alarms shrieked about the lack of oxygen as our son turned blue. Previously, I had worried that I wouldn't notice if a baby in my care stopped breathing. I would always do a double take seeking out a rising and falling chest to confirm life.

NEWS FLASH.

No matter what your profession you can tell when a baby stops breathing. I didn't need a double look. Sam's face and lips went from warm baby pink to deathly blue. Within seconds all colour leached out of him, as an ashen tone crept over his body like a ghostly veil. During these episodes the nurse would open the little porthole to poke and prod Sam, hoping the jostling would encourage him to breathe. As the nurse prodded we leaned forward imploring, "Come on Sam, breathe."

"Just breathe Sammy."

"Please start breathing."

The longer he went and the stronger the blue tinge, the louder our pleading voices merged with the piercing monitor alarms. We weren't sure why these 'apnoeas' (breath holding) were happening but the doctors suspected they were a result of seizures. So an anti-epileptic drug was introduced and Sam was attached to a CPAP machine to help him breathe. This new contraption allowed Sam to initiate his breath before the machine kicked in and supported his lungs to inflate.

Within a few days, Sam started making massive improvements. He no longer needed the CPAP machine and was transferred out of intensive care into the normal special care baby unit. Our little family now occupied a side room where physical barriers became redundant. We could easily pick him up, hold him, talk to him and express our love. We bought our first digital camera and recorded every grimace, cry and expression with the obsession of a new parent.

Soon I was well enough to be discharged. Having enjoyed the flexibility and freedom of being nearby, I now faced going home without my son. I feared that being even a short car journey away from Sam was too far.

What if he started deteriorating and we couldn't get back in time?

How could I be his mum with so much distance between us?

When the time came, my dad was nominated driver. Appearing like an ailing patient, I took the elevator down to the entrance with Tim protectively by my side. The sliding doors swept open as I gulped in the cold October air. With a heavy heart and empty hands, I walked the few steps from the hospital doorway to my dad's warm car, leaving my little boy in his clear box surrounded by strangers.

The short journey produced an onslaught of emotions, with quiet and contained tears. I shuddered as I stepped back into our house; my home suddenly felt empty, bare and slightly cold.

"Let me show you upstairs," my mum exclaimed, keen to point out many thoughtful touches.

"I hired a breast pump for you."

Gratitude and disdain seeped through me in equal measure. I didn't want to need this ghastly machine. When I caught sight of Sam's picture taking pride of place on his chest of drawers, I withered with a sense of loss. Like a flower hankering for water, I wilted a little more and wept.

My wonderful mum had tried to think of everything because she couldn't give me the one thing I wanted, my little boy sleeping soundly in his cot.

That night I tried to wash off the alien feelings swamping me by taking a shower and as I climbed into bed I felt comforted by the familiarity of my own duvet. I was pleased to leave behind the overnight noises and footsteps of the hospital, yet instinctively I recalled the last time I had slept in this bed.

What had happened to my little boy as he lay inside me?
What could I have done differently?

Tim held me as I cried. Leaving the hospital was embodying the distance I felt towards Sam. I found myself

36

living in a land between; suspended in a time where I was unable to see a future or understand the past.

Over the following week, we travelled between our two worlds; home and hospital. Although the journey took only minutes, they felt eons apart. Returning to the ward was like re-entering an unfamiliar alternate universe that held our hopes and lives in the balance. Every night we left and every morning we returned.

Finally, I got the chance to experience breastfeeding. It seemed Sam knew what he was doing more than me and suckled well. It was decidedly more pleasant than having my nipple sporadically pulled by a megaphone. We also tried 'skin to skin'. Undressing Sam we would lie his naked body on my or Tim's bare chest. Studies in Australia had shown this 'kangaroo care' helped recovery and we were prepared to try anything. Feeling Sam's warm plump skin rest on me as his head nestled under my chin felt magical. In our pokey side room looking out on another brick wall it was as though an extra window had been flung open, allowing natural light and fresh air to bathe our lives. As his little frame relaxed and sank into my body I felt the distance between us thaw.

Throughout this time family members visited and many friends phoned or sent cards, flowers, and messaged. Tim's good friend Badger called on the morning of his wedding. Outside life was carrying on; beautiful, wonderful things were happening in the world, while we were hauled up within the walls of the special care baby unit.

Our first experience of parenthood was so different from what we had anticipated or previously witnessed. My sense of isolation wasn't dissipating but rather continued to be magnified. I think I have always felt a little different and

37

separate throughout life, as though I'm the observer of a beautiful dance where everyone else knows the steps except me. Sitting in Sam's little side room I sensed my previously neurotic feelings of being an outsider had finally become a reality. Like a self-fulfilling prophecy, my experience of motherhood had shot off on a completely different trajectory. I was hurtling down an unknown road without a map or companions who had weathered the journey before me.

Emotions trickled through me. New and old feelings appeared bigger and bolder than ever before. I soared with the joy and relief of a positive hearing test, but then plummeted into deep and impenetrable anxiety following the results of an EEG that showed a 'dampening' of activity. The only way I coped with this ebb and flow of emotion was to remain busy and cling to each piece of good news.

Ten days after Sam was born, his nasogastric tube was nearly redundant. Breastfeeding took over and he began gaining weight. Sam was free from any signs of seizures or apnoeas and medication free. We eagerly cajoled the medical staff that there wasn't anything they were doing in hospital that couldn't be done in the comfort of our terraced house.

On Friday 21st October Tim, Sam and I squeezed into our fifth hospital room in two weeks. Home was just a couple of nights and a little weight gain away (Sam, not me). Discharge was within reach and we were determined to grasp it with both hands.

5

Home

"Home is where the heart is."

Pliny the Elder

One of my earliest memories of school is playing in the 'home' area in the corner of the classroom. I would make breakfast on the little plastic cooker, tell my children off for misbehaving and generally boss around my husband. The couple of nights in the special care baby unit's family room felt a little like that, except for the bossing around my husband bit. We had our little corner of the world and busied ourselves with playing family. We tried to act normal and pretended this was life.

For two days we lived and slept in a small, plain room off the main ward of special care baby unit. On the other side of the door people in uniform and hospital trolleys trundled past, whilst inside our belongings were piled up between two single beds and a hospital crib. I looked around at our temporary home and saw everything I held most dear contained within four walls.

By Sunday the medical staff expressed surprise and delight at Sam's progress.

"If I didn't know his history," exclaimed one doctor, "I would have thought I was discharging a normal baby."

His words rang in my ears. I had a normal baby, in our

39

normal family (not strictly true), back to our normal home. Sam was a good size, feeding well, on no medication, no tubes stuck to his face, awake and alert for appropriate periods of time. With all this good news, our hope gathered momentum.

On 23rd October I stood once again at the hospital entrance and waited for a car to pull up. Tim and I strapped in a baby car seat, too happy to argue about the correct position. Our arms were full of gifts, belongings, an appointment to see the consultant, an MRI scan and our son. Again I cried at being discharged but this time tears of joy distorted my view. I sat looking between Sam and the eyes of my husband in the rearview mirror.

Approaching our front door, I stopped by the gate.

"Hold on, I want to take a photo."

Standing on the brink of home suddenly felt momentous, a slither of time that deserved to be captured and remembered. I retrieved our camera and, while Tim balanced bags and belongings between his teeth, I took a photo of a moment I hadn't dared dream of. We stepped inside and the door closed behind us. We were home as a family and in our hearts we clung to the hope that we brought back our miracle baby.

Within hours we were plunged into the unknown world of nappies, feeds, broken sleep and clock watching. In the seclusion a mild sense of unease pervaded. Someone somewhere thought it was perfectly safe to let me care for a beautiful little boy without supervision. We held our son and kissed his cheeks, dissecting every noise and movement. Simple pleasures filled our house as we experienced love and exhaustion like we had never known before.

Tim returned to work a week after we were discharged and my mum swept through our house like a greying Tasmanian devil, with slightly less dust and much more helpfulness. She shopped and cleaned, we chatted and hugged. Relief was palpable as I tried to develop a new pace of life whilst believing our little boy was special and unique.

Days and weeks passed as I made phone calls and wrote emails to explain what had happened. We shared our heartbreak and uncertainty with a generous helping of gratitude at Sam's progress and our hope for a bright future. People were exceedingly positive. Doctors I worked alongside focused on assuring me of the amazing protective nature of a baby's brain, while friends gave a less medicalised but equally enthusiastic assurance that all would be well.

On Sunday 13th November both our family and friends joined us at church to celebrate Sam's dedication. We thanked God for our son and promised to raise him the best we could, loving him and becoming his greatest fans. We had discussed postponing the dedication until after the MRI but decided we were thankful, independent of its results.

The day was alive with my favourite things: people, food, smiles and worship. Tim made himself comfortable at church and perched behind his drum kit to play with the band. We were typically exhausted new parents. Sleep was a long and distant memory setting a cloak of tiredness around us. Even Sam looked bewildered. People travelled from all over to join in celebrating Sam's life and promised to help us raise him. Our smiles portrayed genuine relief and excitement for our family.

A week later, I sat in the small conservatory at the rear of our home, and picked up the phone to call Liz. We had met a few weeks earlier in a crowded room with a dozen other women sporting large bulging bellies. Tim had used the creative excuse of work to avoid attending any antenatal classes, while I decided it was a good way to make new friends. On the first week I spotted Liz and decided she looked more like me than anyone else, and by the end of the sessions we had exchanged phone numbers with plans made to meet again.

We hadn't been in touch since Sam was born and my heart raced as the phone tolled.

"Hello?"

"Hi Liz, it's Rachel from the antenatal class. How are you?"

"Hi Rachel, I'm good thanks."

My hand shook as I nervously retold the story of Sam's birth. What I discovered that day was that Liz would be one of my most level headed and thoughtful allies. She didn't try to persuade me all would be well, nor did she allow me to dwell on my darkest fears. She listened and spoke with kindness.

She had been adamant she was going to have a girl. So I smiled when she told me the tale of Arthur's arrival just three days after Sam. Other than a traumatic delivery as a result of Arthur's decidedly large head, he was delivered healthy and well. Our lighthearted conversation flowed with talk of the things we had in common and we planned the first of many get-togethers with our babies.

From then on, the babies just kept on coming. Paul's wife, Claire, gave birth to Joshua a few days after Sam's dedication, while our friends Rachel and Russell were booked in for a caesarean to deliver their second son. Every direction I turned I was flanked by healthy newborn baby boys.

Sam's six-week check with the consultant came quickly. I walked to the hospital to save on parking and breathlessly handed over his little red book to the receptionist. Before long, a nurse called us in and recorded his weight, height and head circumference. Meanwhile, Tim rushed over from working on

42

the elderly care ward.

"Samuel Wright!" The familiar voice called across the drone of parents and children.

"How are you?" asked Sam's consultant.

We settled into our seats and smiled.

"Good thanks," we chirped, hoping our positivity would be infectious.

After many questions and a thorough examination, the doctor confessed to being delighted that Sam appeared to be tracking objects with his eyes and smiling. The consultant was hopeful and encouraged us that all seemed favourable and maybe, just maybe, Sam had escaped without any major brain damage.

6

Truth: 20th December 2005

"For with much wisdom comes much sorrow;
the more knowledge, the more grief."

Ecclesiastes 1v18

Twenty-four hours before the winter solstice I woke in the dark knowing this was a defining day. Previously, moments of transformation had been unexpected and unpredictable but this cold Tuesday morning before Christmas was destined to become an anniversary. My friend Rachel was booked in for a caesarean section that afternoon, whilst we headed to London to find out more about our son.

We packed a baby bag, loaded up a buggy and, armed with an appointment letter, caught the train and tube towards Hammersmith Hospital. Having both trained and lived in London, the details of the journey were easy. Going over familiar tracks with their well-known landmarks seemed strange. We had loved our student lives in such a vibrant city; going out with friends to the bars, theatres, museums and galleries on our doorstep. The busyness of our lives revolved around how much we could squeeze in. Now every iconic building and railway platform was being viewed from a different perspective. The structures hadn't changed; we had.

Coming out of the tube station we took the short walk to

the hospital. It was a big, old, grand building with facades of modern extensions and elegant foyers. As we walked the corridors, our shoes echoed off the high ceilings and walls of aging paint.

Entering the day ward, we were shown to an old metal bed. I lifted Sam out of his buggy and allowed him to lie on his back and kick. Soon a doctor came and spoke with us, asking all the details of my pregnancy and Sam's delivery. Just before she left we mentioned his head circumference. Concerns had grown over the previous two weeks when we discovered Sam's head circumference had been documented incorrectly. It hadn't followed his centile like his height and weight, but rather it had fallen off the scale and was markedly small. We tried to flippantly excuse it as an anomaly, but the doctor's lack of willingness to disregard this information allowed the worm of doubt occupying my stomach to grow.

Sam was given his sedative, and his body began to relax as the tension in my own muscles mounted. Within an hour, we were following a nurse along a maze of corridors until we reached the MRI suite in the bowels of the hospital.

I kissed Sam goodbye and watched my sleeping son enter the scanning room with more smiling strangers. The nurse directed us to a couple of blue plastic poly chairs. They sat awkwardly, jutting out along the corridor and required us to swing our legs to the side every time a trolley passed. We were surprised that this was deemed the most appropriate place for parents to wait to have their destiny foretold. Like a palm reading, the scan would give us a glimpse of our future. Nonchalantly we talked about nothing important and time ambled past.

When Sam was in the scanner for longer than expected, a battle began in my mind.

Was this a good or bad sign?
What had they found?
Why was it taking so long?
Suddenly the door opened and our doctor approached.
"Well the scan is finished."
Was that a smile of sympathy?
"You can take Sam back to the ward. We will come and explain the results in detail later."

I shot a look at Tim.

"That can't be good news," I whispered. "She would have said if it was good news."

"Don't worry. It means nothing. Let's just wait until we speak to the consultant."

As Sam came round on the ward, I fed him and surrounded him with love. The doctor returned and we played follow my leader through the hospital once more. Our family proceeded along anonymous corridors heading towards the truth. My heart raced and thumped at my chest wall. Tim kept a firm grip of my hand as I silently reminded myself the baby we had grown to love and adore would not change with these results.

The doctor in front of us finally stopped, swung open a door, and showed us into a small office. We entered clinging onto our hopes of a miracle, with our dreams intact. The room resembled a large cupboard, absent of a two-seater sofa or box of tissues. With the small room void of natural light, limited space and haphazard layout, the doctor was required to perch on the edge of a desk as she began to talk.

I sat down, leaving Sam in his buggy beside me, and allowed my eyes to wander towards a brain scan displayed in the corner of the room. Previously, I had witnessed patients receive news, good and bad, but today the image on the screen held the ability to change *my* life forever.

"I'm Doctor Rutherford," the slight woman explained. She introduced her colleague, whom we had seen earlier that day.

"I'm afraid it isn't good news. The scan shows severe brain damage." Her words were spoken lightly, yet the room began to close in. She gently and calmly explained in detail how the scan showed Sam had been very unlucky.

I sat rigidly and gazed across at the scan. I began to see a withered, shrunken brain, with deep darkened rims of space where healthy tissue should have been. She explained Sam's brain damage was both unusual and extensive. Not only had he suffered damage to the white matter but also the grey matter.

"From the scan we can only assume that numerous insults occurred in the time leading up to Sam's birth and then again at delivery," she informed us. Her words became a blur of white noise as my mind drowned out the truth; replaying all the times I may have allowed this catastrophic event to occur.

How had I missed my baby struggling inside me?

How had I carried on singing, stripping wallpaper and going about my daily life, when the fragile being inside me was suffering repeated insults?

What kind of mother was I?

Refocusing on the words being thrown around the room, I brought my mind back to the small office and information I wanted to ignore.

"All parts of his brain are affected. He will live with cerebral palsy... resulting in learning difficulties... as well as physical limitations." There was nothing to say, so we simply nodded, indicating our readiness to hear more.

"He will have complex needs and it seems the areas affecting temperature regulation and vision are particularly damaged."

Tim bravely asked questions and I was surprised at his

47

ability to talk with a steady voice. The doctor remained vague. We weren't told he would never walk, talk or eat, but it was indicated that each of these things was in jeopardy.

It was as though the doctor conjured up a paintbrush dripping with brilliant white emulsion and began covering the wall of our future. What had once displayed vivid colourful strokes of our hopes, dreams and future plans, was being abruptly erased. The blank canvas that remained felt daunting rather than full of potential. Nothing could be assumed, and nothing could be expected. Our medical backgrounds brought insight into the myriad of potential complications.

Sometimes ignorance is bliss.

A bomb had exploded in the middle of our lives splintering our world into thousands of tiny pieces. Like walking wounded, we staggered out of the hospital holding onto each other, dazed and bewildered. The words spoken over us rang in our ears. As reality began to sink in, I was surprised at the magnitude of my shock. I simply hadn't prepared myself for hearing my little boy had profound brain damage.

Outside, I tucked a blanket around Sam to ward off the bleak and icy day. Cars raced past on the busy London road in front of the hospital as I stood with my husband. Holding each other, we began to weep. Our minds raced, while our nerves felt deadened. Having peeled ourselves apart, we had the difficult task of calling our parents.

Once again, we cut into the ordinary days of our loved ones with a life changing revelation. Through broken words and tears, we explained what the doctor had said. Heartbreak was tangible on both ends of the phone line.

As we ambled towards White City tube, busy commuters weaved in and around us hurriedly trying to get home. Following the sea of people migrating towards the underground, we wished we had brought a car. Reaching the gaping entrance of the tube, we quickly hustled through the turnstiles. The train arrived and I looked up at the greying sky. We lifted the buggy off the platform before the doors closed behind us and with spluttering jerks headed for the tunnel.

Few words littered our tube journey. Tim held my hand or shoulder and kept contact the whole way. I began to comprehend the extent of the assumptions I had made whilst carrying Sam. So many dreams and plans had sprouted as my baby grew in my womb.

Once we had boarded our busy rush hour train, we squeezed the buggy to one side desperately avoiding the disapproving looks of commuters. Nothing could make our day worse. As we sat close together and quietly talked, we started to unpack the implications of the truth. We noticed that rather than the uncertainty of whether our son might go to university we were left wondering if he would ever communicate, sit, walk, eat or see.

In a single breath nothing could be assumed; my worm of doubt was replaced with a stone of uncertainty. As the emotional elements of our reality lay bare before us, I discovered I would need a backpack to carry them all around. Wherever I went, no matter what we did, my backpack of emotions was there, varying in burden and inconvenience, but ever present.

I had to identify and lay down all my previous expectations and start with a clean sheet. I could remain hopeful and work towards the unexpected, but in order to manage my feelings I decided to anticipate nothing. It was harder and more draining to be repeatedly disappointed, to compare life with what should or could have been.

All of the 'first' milestones a parent looks forward to, takes photos of and posts on Facebook had been stolen from us. I had left them in a small office in the depths of Hammersmith Hospital, along with my hopes. I was going to have to work out a new selection of 'firsts' that I could celebrate, unique to the world I would occupy with my family.

I had to live in a new normal.

As we got closer to home my phone beeped with the news that Rachel and Russell's little boy had been born by caesarean section.

Mother and baby were well.

I began weeping again.

After visiting Rachel's newborn son and sharing our news, we came home and crawled into bed. Through the night I woke and fed Sam as usual. My emotions were raw, and the idea of cowering in a corner and weeping uncontrollably was very appealing. Every train of thought I had led me to a dead-end. I couldn't see the simplest detail of my future. For the early morning feed I went back to bed and propped myself up with pillows. Tim woke beside me.

"Morning," I said, wondering if my words sounded as hollow as I felt.

"Are you calling work or are you going to go in?"

"I think I'll go in. I don't want to spend ages trying to get through to my consultant like yesterday. If I go in early I can talk to her and come straight home."

"What are you going to say?" We both glanced at Sam and became suddenly protective.

"I'll tell her what happened yesterday and that I'm not fit to work. If she gives me the next couple of days off, I can go back after next week's annual leave."

As Tim silently began to get ready, I bumbled around in my dressing gown sorting Sam and making tea. Tim chose to dress smartly and maintain a level of professionalism. He handled difficult situations every day but the impending conversation would require a level of vulnerability he didn't normally take to work.

After we kissed goodbye, I sat on the sofa trying to play with Sam and imagined Tim planning his words on his walk to work.

Thirty minutes later, my phone rang and I was surprised to see Tim's number flash up.

"Hello?"

"Hi, I can't talk long I'm on the ward."

"What?"

"I met the consultant in the hospital foyer and explained what had happened. I said I wasn't fit to work but she said it is too late to get cover."

"You're kidding!"

"No, she says I need to do my on-call so I won't be home until ten o'clock tonight. I'm so, so, sorry… but I need to go."

I could tell by the tone of Tim's voice he was close to tears and sitting on a busy ward. He had already shut down in order to manage the day ahead of him.

I knew he wanted to be at home.

I knew I needed him.

"Ok," came my equally controlled reply.

"Call your mum straight away. I know she'll come see you. I'm sorry. My annual leave starts tonight. We just have to get through today and then we can do Christmas together."

"All right, I hope you aren't too busy. Love you, bye."

Hanging up the phone I looked down at Sam. Here was my beautiful boy and yet grief hung thick in the air. The day ahead looked impossible and I couldn't imagine how hard it would be for Tim. I called Mum and explained what had happened, then I sat lifeless on the sofa. It was over two hours before I heard Mum's knock at the door. I had barely moved. Rising from the sofa holding Sam, the weight of the truth lay heavily in my arms.

Part 2
A New Normal

7

A New Year: 1st January 2006

"Hope smiles from the threshold of the year to come,
Whispering 'it will be happier'..."

Alfred Tennyson

Droplets of similarity ran between New Years' Eve in 2006 and 2005. A year earlier we had parked our hired camper van in Daintree National Park, Australia. We cooked the best meal possible on a couple of gas hobs, then spent the evening alone drinking and talking. The next morning, we rose early to see the sun rise off Cape Tribulation, agreeing we would stay in our nightwear and head back to bed afterwards. With my camera I captured an image of Tim silhouetted against the rising sun off the Coral Sea. Standing in his theatre blue pyjamas he appeared relaxed and expectant, with his hands resting upon his head.

The poignancy of this picture heightened with the passing year as I was reminded that the view around each corner is hidden. I have no periscope for life. All I can do is live in today, soaking up each moment, creating precious jewels of memory to store away and admire at any time.

One year later we were again alone, together and sharing a meal. We talked about life, what had passed, and what lay ahead. We had swapped the golden sandy beaches of the Australian east coast for the Thames Estuary and Kent's idyllic power station skyline. Last year we had gone for a run in the tropical rain of Northern Australia. This year I waited up for Tim to return home after being on-call. Last year we felt beautifully alone, enjoying new experiences and places with a year of unknowns stretching out in front of us. This year our son slept in his cot upstairs, as a different kind of solitude enwrapped us.

Sitting on the sofa, I shed a few tears as I began to unravel the implications of Sam's cerebral palsy. The future was different; void of the things we had once valued and loved. The new and challenging experiences that had once filled us up were now replaced with unforeseen problems and trials. My rose tinted glasses had been swapped for heavy dark specs.

Life had changed.

In those wintery months, I gazed at Sam and wondered if it was all a big mistake. The conflict between what I could see and what I had been told was immense. Sammy didn't look different to his friends. I held my beautiful baby and felt overwhelmed with love and gratitude. I learnt nursery rhymes with gusto and playfully nibbled Sam's fingers, determined to make my boy smile.

The allure of my baby was no less than anyone else's. I started conversations with old ladies staring into his pushchair as they doted on his sparkling blue eyes and soft, chunky cheeks. He created havoc and delight in equal measure, while my emotions and questions stayed obediently tucked away. Differences seemed absent and his appearance normal. He would lie, kick, smile, coo and laugh with as much delight as any other adorable baby.

Like everyone else, I worked towards milestones such as leaving the house before lunchtime. With growing confidence I progressed to the dizzy height of brushing my hair and teeth before I crossed the doorstep to embrace the outside world. My child's unknown future paled into insignificance when faced with his odorous nappies and projectile vomiting that managed to reach places normally only cleaned on an annual basis.

When I was pregnant, people tried to warn me about the chaos of a newborn. In a perverse way, I now enjoy seeing the change in the confident 'How hard can it be?' eyes of a woman during her first pregnancy. The transformation into the sleep deprived, tearful eyes of a desperate woman wondering how something so small can cause so much mayhem is universal. Like every other woman I know, I wasn't fully prepared for the military operation required to get through a twenty-four hour period with a newborn. The simplest of tasks required mission statements and detailed precision planning. Getting out of the house started at least two hours before the estimated time of departure and demanded more equipment than the contents of a NASA space station.

One unremarkable morning, I collected the post from the doormat and flicked through the envelopes. Surreptitiously within them was the hospital letter from Sam's scan; I sat at the bottom of the stairs to read. A cold breeze swept through my home and joy of motherhood. Its words tumbled from the page and landed on my lap where they mingled with my falling tears. My hands shook as I held the darkness in black and white markings on a page. It read:

'Widespread infarction of parenchymal white matter... most marked posteriorly but involved all regions of the brain... some involvement of the basal ganglia with atrophy and abnormal signal intensity with the thalamus. Myelination... was absent.'

Long words with negative add-ons danced across my

mind, jeering and taunting me. I suspected the more I understood, the worse it sounded. I looked up from my position on the stairs to see my son lying on his back, the baby gym above him as his fingers played delicately in front of his mouth.

How could such perfection be communicated in such a damning way?

Physically I rose, leaving my spirit on the floor. I swept Sam into my arms and sobbed as his sweet baby smell penetrated my sadness. It seems there is nothing funnier than Mummy crying, so Sam laughed. Looking at him, a smile punctured my tears; this boy could not be confined to black marks on a page. I continued with my duties, drained and fragile. It was days before I fully collected myself from the bottom step and the uninvited darkness lifted.

In between Sam's appointments and therapy sessions I avoided 'normal' baby groups. Whereas before I had loved being part of a community, getting energy from banter and friendships, suddenly old friendships had an air of unease. Some conversations no longer flowed, but stuttered and faltered. Being around both strangers and friends became a minefield.

So instead I attended the local toy library that holds coffee mornings for parents of disabled children. The first time I entered the sliding doors of the Lighthouse Child Development Centre, my heart pounded as my sweaty palms clung tightly to Sam's car seat.

"Good morning." A lady rose from her chair. "I'm Judy, nice to meet you."

"Hi." I smiled. "I'm Rachel and this is Sammy."

The welcome was warm and unconditional, and the atmosphere relaxed. Although I sat amidst strangers I felt amongst friends. It wasn't easy accepting my place in this group but it was considerably easier than times with other mums and painful comparisons.

At the toy library no awkward questions were asked, but rather our conversation was frank and jovial. Sam was doted over by people who were travelling down a road similar to mine. Knowing they understood firsthand what I was experiencing flooded me with relief.

8

Community, God and Healing

"Shadrach, Meshach and Abednego replied, 'If we are thrown into the
blazing furnace, the God we serve is able to deliver us from it...
But even if he does not... we will not serve your gods or worship the image of
gold you have set.'"

Daniel 3v16-18

The most important community of people in my life is church. Being part of a church is part of me, and a rhythm in my week. Whether in someone's living room, an ornate building, or school hall, my memories are littered with numerous expressions of church. Sitting on the hard pews next to my Grandma Hessie wearing our Sunday best was made that much sweeter knowing the surrounding old ladies had a habit of slipping 10p in my hand after the service.

Growing up, our arrival at church caused quite a stir when all seven members of our family oozed out of a Mini (seat belts and car seats not an option). The noise and mild chaos continued in the relaxed service, held in a community centre. When we moved to Southend we left a large, young, Anglican church we attended as students in London and joined a much smaller family-centred Baptist church. The people quickly became our friends and the Sunday morning routine continued.

My attempts to be on time, however, were repeatedly

thwarted by Sam. Trying to gather the various items required to last two hours out of the house, along with the obligatory poo Sam deposited just as we were leaving, stumped me every time. Pre-baby, I joined Tim early as he played the drums and I sang as part of the music team. Post-baby, Sam and I often stormed into the service a little after it had started. Thankfully, a wonderful person, such as Maggie, would invariably arrive slightly later, applying much needed balm to my guilty sense of tardiness.

After the service, friends gathered around us, enquiring about Sam's progress. Many would provide gentle reassurance by revealing they were still praying. I tried to shrug off a sense that their prayers camouflaged dissatisfaction about the difficult questions Sam's cerebral palsy posed.

I wanted my baby to be fixed; a desire that came not from my faith, but from being a mother. The deep longing parents have to heal and restore is universal. I have many friends who have raised thousands of pounds to fly to another country in the hope of an alternative therapy and potential miracle. The desperation to make our children better, how we had hoped and expected, is strong and deep. The feelings, issues and values highlighted are the same. Coming to a place of acceptance and wholeness is hard, with or without a faith.

Since I was a teenager, I had developed an uncomfortable relationship with the idea of healing. Aged only fifteen I suffered with chronic fatigue syndrome for over a year. When the prayers of our church elders didn't result in healing, they concluded that my illness was directly related to the sin of my parents, and my lack of healing a consequence of their lack of faith. Since that time, although I clung onto the belief of a miraculous God, I never prayed for or expected healing in the

60

same way.

Whilst in Uganda the issue of healing came to the forefront of my faith again. I found myself in church having prayer for my asthma, a condition I have lived with since childhood. I stood on the plain concrete floor of our thriving church in Kampala, as music blared and harmonious singing circulated overhead. I stood still with my eyes closed and heart open to a miracle (sounds weird, I know). I was expectant. I had no weird sensations, no burning heat in my lungs or visions of angels, but I believed I was healed.

After work the next day, Tim and I went for a run, as usual, and I questioned whether I should take my inhaler. If I even held my inhaler, just in case, surely I wasn't demonstrating faith in having been healed. So I headed out with a nervous husband and no inhaler.

I was confident and optimistic, and the run was a success. No wheezing, no tightness, and a fully healed pair of lungs were celebrated. I was amazed, delighted and thankful. The following day we opted to sort out the filing at the clinic; a daunting and dusty task. Within fifteen minutes I was sneezing and half an hour later my lungs were ragged, as I wheezed and struggled to breathe. Anger raged within me, I was devastated.

"Can you go and get my inhaler?" I grunted to my husband.

Prayer had failed.

What if it was all nonsense?

The faith I had built up over the last twenty-odd years crumbled around me.

Was it all a farce?

Just a load of super-spiritual claptrap manipulated and twisted to make me feel better?

Tim and I talked for hours, our roles suddenly reversed.

61

Traditionally, I had been the one with the stronger, more vocal faith. Now, I was asking Tim questions. I wrote an email to our minister back home, and his response clarified what I didn't believe about healing.

His reply told me I needed to keep praying. He suggested I should insist on being healed, because God always wants to heal. Healing is always His desire, he explained, and anything else is not what God wants. Sickness isn't part of God's plan, so as a Christian I should believe in my right to be healed.

Although the email was full of love and support, I was immediately uncomfortable with my minister's response. Always insisting and believing that healing was a 'right' felt like a dangerous path that robs death of peace because it is never timely or good. I also felt uncomfortable with seeing physical perfection as Godly. History reveals many harrowing stories of regimes focused on eradicating imperfection from the human race. Surely my faith should be about loving those who are weak, not eradicating weakness. The greatest asset of being human is our capacity to care for the vulnerable and value life in its brokenness.

Living on the outskirts of a large Kampala slum, insisting my asthma was healed began to feel outrageous. Could I really believe that God ought to ensure only good things happen to me (that is good things as I prescribed them). I know those without a faith often blame God when life takes a tumble.

As I sat in our walled garden with the noises of the slum creeping over our boundaries, I decided my asthma didn't need healing. I had an inhaler and it worked a treat. If a couple of hundred years ago someone had whipped out an inhaler to help a wheezing onlooker, everyone would have called it a miracle.

Does it stop being a miracle because I know how it works?
Is the birth of a baby any less miraculous because I

understand fragments of the process?

I am reminded of a tale told many times before about a man stranded up a tree, trapped by floods who prays to God.

"Heavenly Father, save me from this flood. Show your mighty hand and save your servant from certain death," the man bleats.

"Yes, my child," booms God, (because He either thunders or whispers) "I promise I will save you."

So, the man sits and waits, ready to be rescued. After a while perched in the tree a rescue boat comes by and offers him a lift to safety.

"No, don't worry about me. You go rescue someone else. God has this covered," shouts the man over the wind and rain.

The floodwaters rise, but the man remains confident that he heard God speak and will be rescued. In the distance, he hears the sound of propellers, the water now only a few centimetres from his branch of safety.

"Grab onto the rope," bellows a man in a helicopter hovering overhead. Frantically, the man shakes his hands like the leaves clinging onto his branch.

"No. I'm trusting God. Go save someone else," he yells back.

"Tie the rope around your waist or you will drown," screams the frustrated rescuer.

"NO! NO! God is my saviour. He promised." Begrudgingly, the helicopter moves on to rescue others more willing to get on board.

Minutes later, the man is swept to his death in the floods.

His eyes open in heaven, portraying indignation and fury.

"Why didn't you save me?" implores the man. "I trusted you and you failed me."

63

Exasperated, God raises his eyebrows and replies, "I sent you a boat and a helicopter and you turned them both down. What more did you want?"

All around me people were dying for reasons that simply would not have been the case in the UK. I have no idea why, but I am privileged with the NHS, and an inhaler. I don't blame God for the injustices, poverty and disease I saw ravaging people I cared about. I clearly saw my own Western greed for cheap products and a lavish lifestyle, colluding with corruption to force impoverished countries into a desperate mess.

Was my birthplace and inhaler my miracle?

I hated the inequality my friends in Kampala experienced, but why was I getting despondent about not being healed of something I had treatment for? My problems were comparatively so very small. The simple fact is that life and death are a painful, messy business in Uganda and for many, comfort stems from believing that a higher being holds everything together. For me, my faith began posing more questions and providing fewer answers. Life wasn't neatly parcelled up; I couldn't pretend to live in a black and white world, there were too many hues of grey.

Trusting in a higher power was now founded on believing that life is full of unexplained, unknown and unseen things that were beyond my understanding. Through the remainder of my time in Uganda and then in New Zealand, I pieced together the remnants of my faith and created something new. It evolved into something raw, less neat, but more resilient. When all the emotions of my faith had evaporated, I chose to believe in an unremarkable Jew that walked this earth a couple of thousand years ago. It sounded crazy, but managed to resonate as true.

When Sam was born, I was thankful that I didn't need to

shoulder the guilt of him not being healed. I didn't see healing as the only goodness in my life, although I will admit I had no idea what God was playing at. I knew good people had bad things happen to them all the time. All of us will die and our bodies are prone to failing; everyone is broken.

I wanted Sam to be healed more than anyone else. His disability crushed me, changed my world and my dreams. This wasn't a cold that would pass; Sam's disability would be a defining feature of his life. There was nothing I wanted more than God to make it how I had expected it to be, yet when the scan showed that Sam had not been healed, Tim and I made the decision to stop praying for such a healing.

My spiritual, psychological and physical energy was close to empty. I couldn't afford to spend any of it hoping my son was something he wasn't. Faith wasn't about believing things would get better; cajoling, confessing or pleading for healing. Faith became living the worst-case scenario and still trusting in God, no matter what. It was founded on believing that He is bigger than every circumstance and that goodness, hope and love could be present whether I was living my most wonderful dreams or darkest nightmare.

I focused on accepting, loving and responding to Sam's needs. I had full confidence that God could see my broken heart and knew my deepest thoughts and feelings. I began to see restoration as getting to the point where I could look at Sam in all his wholeness and not hurt.

9

A Parable

There was once a father who loved his son.

When the son was eight years old he contracted meningitis. As a result, he suffered brain damage that affected his lower limbs and speech. From that day on his father cared for his every need.

Because the father dearly loved his son, his care overflowed with compassion and tenderness. Each morning he woke in the quiet of the house, dressed and knelt by his bed to pray for his son's healing. His heart longed for his son to enjoy life as he had done before he became sick.

As the days passed the passion in the father's voice didn't fade when he called on God for healing. Then each day he helped his son get up, dressed him and enabled him to have many of the opportunities afforded to other children.

There were days when the burden of care was difficult and overwhelming, but the father was determined not to show the strain. He dedicated himself to caring, the smile on his face never portraying the heaviness in his heart.

The son's peers grew from boys to men. They rose up to look the father in his eyes, as they talked to him of their futures and careers. The father listened intently with a firm smile and silent sadness. Each morning he continued to pray and each day he watched his son, contained within a wheelchair, dependent on care, limited by stairs and hampered by prejudice.

One morning the father rose to pray only to learn that his son had died.

Within days, he was standing by his dear son's grave. The rain that soaked his hair trickled down his face and mingled with his free-flowing tears. The brave smile had disappeared, allowing the raw pain of the last twenty years to be exposed.

Amidst his grief, the father was comforted that finally his son was whole. He had so longed for his son to be healed, and now he believed he finally was. He found solace in imagining his son running and smiling in the beauty and eternity of heaven.

For years the father visited his son's grave, until one day he too died and found himself opening his eyes to the beauty of heaven. His heart swelled at the excitement of seeing his son in all his wholeness.

As his eyes came in to focus, he found himself gazing into the unforgettable brilliance of his son's dazzling green eyes. He held his gaze, not wanting to look away, captured by the experience of being able to look straight across into his son's face. Finally they looked eye to eye. Their smiles grew and the laughing began as they embraced each other once again.

As the father slowly withdrew from the embrace, he noticed that he wasn't in fact standing, but sitting opposite his son. He looked down and his spirit stilled. He realised his son was sitting in his wheelchair. Like the sun slowly lighting the land at dawn, he became aware that he too was confined to a wheelchair. With confusion in his eyes, he looked up again at his son who hadn't stopped smiling. Without a word from his father, the son began to speak.

"Dad, welcome to heaven. You'll love it here. Don't worry about the wheelchair it doesn't stop you enjoying all the best of living. Here we don't value independence because it's all about interdependence. No one is burdened with care, as we all help one another, living as God created us to be; part of one community, his family. No one is in need, because we share. No one is left out, because we are inclusive. There are no disabilities because they only exist when the world does not accommodate the need. Everything God is passionate about is here; peace, joy, hope, love and faithfulness."

The father looked around heaven in amazement and with fresh understanding. Vulnerability wasn't a weakness, but an opportunity to love and serve. All around he saw every need being supported by others in the community. This world was alive with colour, smells and noise. Everywhere people signed as they talked, there were no stairs, inaccessible places or isolation. It seemed no burden was too heavy to bear.

Everywhere he looked there was serving with laughter and love without limits.

Finally the father spoke. "So this is heaven, this is healing."

10

Tim's Story

First Day: 1st February 2006

"The journey in between what you once were and who you are now becoming is where the dance of life really takes place."

Unknown

Standing in my dressing gown with Sam perched on my hip Tim kissed us both goodbye. Closing the white u-PVC door to lock in the warmth, Tim raised his collar and braced himself for the short trudge to work.

It was a typical morning and routine walk. A tinge of envy crept over him as he longed for the familiar comfort of slippers and a well heated home. Looking back over his shoulder he glimpsed his family standing in the 1920s bay window.

Am I really old enough to be a husband, father, doctor and have a mortgage? he wondered.

The sense of rancour at leaving home was normally short lived. The prospect of a day with nappies, feeding and baby groups sounded about as much fun as watching someone else eat a curry; although a day of cuddles, TV and the solitude of home would be very welcome on this particular day.

The familiar sound of brown leather boots as they

ricocheted off the paving slabs set a reassuring rhythm. Today the journey to work felt longer, greater, and more arduous, as with each step Tim traversed the gulf between being a father and doctor. This morning the transformation warranted a few more strides, as the chasm between his two selves felt greater than ever before.

Crossing the road, Tim subconsciously cut corners to maintain the shortest route. He aimlessly allowed his mind to veer off course and wander down a trail of memories. The stale monotony of his walk to work was uninterrupted, while life and its orientation had changed forever. Like the earth, suddenly opting for a different route around the sun, his world had changed its orbit. Untold triggers had catalysed a chain reaction of consequences, with universal implications impossible to comprehend.

So he stuck to what was familiar.

God be with Rachel and Sam today.
Watch over them and protect them.

Anxiety rose. *Stick to what is familiar.*

Lord, let the people they meet be sensitive and not say anything stupid.
Help Rachel not cry.
I pray Sam doesn't cry too much causing Rachel to cry.

His stomach tightened. *Stick to what is familiar.*

Lord, help me today. Be with me; protect me.
Let no one say anything insensitive.
And Lord, help me not cry today.

It felt like the blink of an eye before the high rise of the hospital loomed and the cold air of the street was replaced with its warm bleached environment. Stepping towards another first day, he anticipated the orientation to be an unceremonious affair. Striding across the polished clinical floors, he stopped momentarily to allow a wheelchair to pass, laden with an old man in a dressing gown and accompanied by a smiling porter. Using this momentary pause, he tried to boost his confidence by concentrating on the wealth of experience gained through practicing medicine on three different continents.

Once on the ward his smile became more genuine as he greeted colleagues and created small talk. The camaraderie of a first day was much like a university fresher's week, but with less lunchtime drinking and fewer outbreaks of acne. The long awaited photocopied A4 sheet of paper started being passed around as the gentle chatter subsided while everyone tried to figure out how the on-calls worked. Soon groans were heard as bank holidays disappeared, along with Easter and birthdays. Before long someone was weaving through their co-workers politely groveling, desperate to try and swap an on-call so they could attend a family wedding.

After analysing the cryptic timetable, Tim followed the gaggle of doctors to be shown around by a senior midwife.

"First I'll take you to the antenatal and postnatal ward," she instructed after a brief introduction. "Then we'll finish up on labour ward. You'll be seeing patients in all these areas, as well as theatre and the gynaecology ward."

How can I be back here so soon? Staying focused and professional, Tim tried to be reassured by the familiarity of hospital life.

It's still patients, on wards, requiring care and doctors. Except many of these patients weren't sick they were just having babies: pink, bouncy and healthy babies.

The tour continued with relative ease as Tim focused on the information being given. Then the doors of the labour ward were swept open and the air thickened. Progressing down the corridor Tim's heart began to beat violently against his chest as the midwife stopped and turned to her right. With the same mindless repetition used to butter a slice of bread, she effortlessly opened a door.

"And this is the Butterfly Suite or Bereavement Suite. We bring women and their families here if they are bereaved or expected to have a poor outcome," she announced.

A stream of junior doctors seeped in through the doors, 'oohing' and 'aahing' as they went.

"As you can see it is a self-contained unit with its own kitchenette, shower, double bed and sofa..."

The midwife's voice trailed off as she disappeared into the room and slightly out of earshot. Quickly, Tim manoeuvred out of sync with his colleagues, side-stepping the doorway and looking up at the surprised face of another doctor,

"It's ok." He smiled. "I don't need to go in. I've been here before."

Moving back he indicated with his hand their right to step inside, and there he waited: on the edge of the doorway, on the cusp of his nightmares. As colleagues smiled and nodded with approval at the fantastic facilities, no words could explain Tim's emotions as experienced within those four walls. Where they saw a double bed, Tim reminisced about the whispered words shared in the dark; talk of death, grief and the future had sliced the night. The homely bedside cabinet would look bare without an oversized mechanical breast pump and an ill-developed Polaroid photo of Sam strapped to a ventilator.

Tim momentarily avoided the visual triggers of the Butterfly Suite on that first day, knowing he wouldn't be able to avoid a catalogue of painful reminders. Memories secured in his mind could be triggered, exposing a wave of emotions he feared would be impossible to contain. Yet before long the new pace and rhythm of obstetrics and gynaecology easily filled his days at work.

Most shifts passed with scenarios distant enough from his own. Then, the first time he was asked to assist in theatre that distance became perilously thin. Suddenly, only a hair's breadth separated life and work.

Getting dressed into freshly pressed blues, opening the doors of the theatre and stepping inside was like stepping back in time. A glance to the left revealed the young couple eager to meet their first baby. Surrounded by unfamiliar machines, they chatted anxiously, keen to fill time.

"You can come this way," an overly helpful midwife instructed, gesturing with her hand. She was garbed up and ready to go.

Tim hoped the small pale theatre mask hid the tension around his lips as the operation got underway. Concentrating hard he kept pace, following instructions with relative ease until things started to cause concern. The atmosphere in the theatre stilled. Voices became hushed, as instructions were barked and the pace of work quickened in line with his pulse. For a moment Tim raised his head and glanced across at the resuscitaire, the very same place he watched his son lie, blue and lifeless. Squeezing his eyes shut, he reminded himself to breathe.

"Will you please stand closer!" barked the midwife.

Blinking to try and dispel the vibrant flashback, Tim's breath quickened as his heart suddenly felt too large for his chest. Realising he had inched away from the table and patient, he stepped forward. Anxiety continued to rise, like the strident whistle of a kettle as it grows louder, demanding attention.

This has got to be okay.

Beads of sweat, unable to be wiped away, settled uncomfortably on Tim's upper lip.

"Will you please concentrate and stand closer." The snarled instruction was repeated.

Trying not to flinch, Tim glanced up at the berating midwife and wondered how he could possibly explain his feelings. He stared back, hoping that if she just looked into his eyes she may somehow understand the memories and thoughts being wrestled under control.

This has got to be ok.

Then seemingly in a flash, the tension was shattered as a baby was lifted, a cord cut and a cry heard. A unified sigh of relief resounded around the theatre. Like the still after a storm, fear was forgotten in an instant, as though nothing untoward had happened.

He sighed.

Many times Tim was required to return to the landscape of his nightmares. Fearful that a tide of emotions may follow, he never revealed the memories he fought, nor the feelings that swamped. Several times he watched the tension rise and fear escalating, yet each time a family left, whole and well. It never appeared to match the complexity of his own life.

Each day he girded himself for what lay ahead, before the ritualistic regularity of the ward and persistent duties distracted him from his memories. The gentle stroll home provided just enough time to silently weep away the emotions accrued through the day before he was back at the white u-PVC door.

"Hello, I'm home. How was your day?" he asked with a kiss.

"You look about as good as I feel," came my encouraging reply.

Drained, Tim smiled. "Glad to see you are out of your dressing gown."

It was good to be home.

11

Running and Praying

"I will learn, I will learn to love the skies I'm under."
Mumford and Sons (Hopeless Wanderer)

As the heavy fog lifted on my role as a mother, the landscape around me remained unclear but I did my best. I learnt the baby shuffle, swaying my hips side to side to soothe and calm my son. For good measure, I added the ability to speak incessantly in a high-pitched tone. Yet as I looked around and ahead untold assumptions rose like mountains on the horizon. I could no longer see the milestones of my son's life; our future's map appeared void of landmarks.

My son was beautiful, small, chubby and seemingly normal. I gazed at him and juggled feelings of limitless love and boundless unknowns. Like any mum, I was learning to live with the topsy-turvy world of my life revolving around another person. Someone now pre-occupied me in a completely unique way. I began to love my baby as I had never loved before.

I enjoyed spending time with Sam. We would go off to baby yoga and massage, merrily copying the techniques. At home in his little bedroom, we lay together on the laminate floor. His head resting gently on my chest, we lay silent and connected, allowing our breaths to rise and fall in the quietness of our yellow, sunlit room.

We listened to music, danced and laughed together. Sam loved being swung around, so we would swirl and prance as I joined him with squealing pleasure. Sam has the dirtiest snigger. It starts in the pit of his stomach and finishes at the tips of his fingers and toes, as a cheeky grin lights up his face. Helplessly I soon heard my own laughter mingling with his chortles.

Amidst the demands of motherhood and the emotional roller coaster of disability, previous rhythms of my day and faith fell away. Where prayer had once been a regular part of life, in those early months it was squeezed into pre-defined times as my duties consumed me. Once, I tried to pray kneeling by my bed but it simply resulted in tears. I didn't have the energy to pray with truth and openness. So I stuck to meal times and being grateful for my food.

My body also felt alien. My new caesarean scar sat alongside my appendix scar, with their new friend 'Stretch Marks' streaking across my abdomen like bright blue claws. Eventually I saw the need to get myself back on track. I needed a spiritual and physical overhaul. I had stopped recognising myself in the mirror and in my head. I wanted to start feeling like me again, whoever that was.

Before Sam was born I had the habit of occasionally running. I dreamed of being a refined athlete, coordinated and elegant, stepping out in pristine lycra ready to overtake any burly middle-aged man I encountered; a bit like Florence Nightingale crossed with Lara Croft from Tomb Raider. Sadly, the reality was a slightly smelly, dishevelled woman huffing and puffing along the pavement with a bright purple, sweaty face.

Slipping into my trainers and closing the door behind me felt liberating, even if my mileage had dramatically reduced. It was satisfying to run again, although I still hated the first fifteen minutes, when my feet felt weighed down and lungs ready to burst. My padded soles bounced off the paving slabs as I headed toward the seafront, with music pounding in my ears. Once I reached the sea wall, I veered right. My breathing found its rhythm and I reflected that my life felt like I had gone for a run to the beach, only to be propelled down a dead end. My experiences in Uganda and New Zealand were like seeing the waves and tasting the salty air, but then having my ankles shackled so it was just out of reach. I had been given a glimpse of a life I wanted; a way of living I found both invigorating and abundant, before it was abruptly taken from view.

I felt duped and tricked.

Why did Tim and I have a desire to work and live abroad?

Sam's birth and resulting disability stopped us in our tracks. Living and working in a developing country was not an option. Our dreams would only ever be dreams. Trapped, I was left standing not knowing where to turn. As I continued running I allowed the rain to hide my tears and the wind carry my screams. Looking at the dark clouds above me I desperately wanted a change in the skyline so I began to pray.

Prayer and meditation means different things to different people. For many it focuses on a higher being, something or someone beyond us. As I ran and struggled to pray, I drew comfort from the stories of a Jew a couple of thousand years ago. I read of Jesus' agony as he called out to his Father before his death and pleaded for his future to be different. His prayers were real, raw and gut-wrenching. I felt satisfied my God wouldn't be distressed by my snot filled, tear stained face.

With time, my fitness slowly improved and the tone of my prayers changed too. Much like Jesus and his young mother before him, I came to a place of saying, 'Your will be done.' After expressing my dreams, emotions and fears with honesty, I sought contentment and peace.

77

Growing up, my Sunday school teacher taught me the story of King David. She told me that God doesn't look at our outward appearance, he looks at our heart. Outwardly, my sweat stained and matted hair matched my reddened face and rasping breath, yet inside good things were happening to my body. My muscles strengthened and heart pounded. Stuff I couldn't see, more important than my blotchy appearance, was improving my health and eventually my head.

Gradually I discovered a new way of looking at Sam; maybe he was more whole than me. Maybe we were both broken, both disabled but in different ways. I could run along the seafront appearing athletic, but my life could be just as crippled by resentment, envy and self-importance.

I jogged, prayed and cried. My muscles became stronger and my vision clearer. With so much time focused on Sam's physical healing, I was missing out on my own. I wanted to press past the pain of circumstances into contentment. Life tasted sweeter when I was no longer struggling against the circumstances of life.

With the passing of time, I stopped focusing on the pavement in front of me, lifted my head and prayed differently. I stopped wanting the weather to change or the view to be different. Instead I prepared to dress more appropriately and appreciate where I was. I began to learn to love the skies I was under.

I had been so consumed with a sense of being restricted and tied down that I was missing the charm of where I was. I became determined to appreciate the waves crashing over the sea wall and the views across the estuary, as boats lay leaning awkwardly on their side. With time, I began to breathe in the beautiful vista before me as I tried to stop hankering after the scenery of my dreams.

12

Words

"The words of the reckless pierce like swords,
but the tongue of the wise brings healing."

Proverbs 12:18

As the sun warmed up 2006 we dared to dream of paddling pools and ice cream. Sam's peers began to sit, roll and grasp, leaving him smiling and cooing in return. He no longer blended in. Our future was intrinsically and unmistakably different to those around us.

My friends diligently documented the milestones of their little ones, arranging play dates and baby groups. Meanwhile I was going to ever more hospital appointments and chasing therapists. Sam was nearly five months old before a physiotherapist visited our home, it seemed we had slipped through the net being discharged at the weekend. Whilst trying to come to terms with Sam's disability, I started having to attend therapy sessions focused on identifying his failures and developing therapies to address them. I couldn't bury my head in the sand at the lack of progress I was seeing; instead I had to face reality.

Soon it was only at home that my family felt normal. My emotions would have coped much better if I didn't have to see other babies and all they could do. My little boy was adorable and easy to love, but I still struggled against my own expectations and what I saw around me.

Sam began to stand out. Sitting in his pushchair or high chair, I needed to roll up towels to keep him upright. His head rolled and flopped about as he struggled to keep it under control. In every position, Sam slumped like a grumpy teenager while the babies we met played bolt upright with completely straight spines having apparently qualified from their postural etiquette lessons.

When I lifted my friends' children, I noticed they held themselves and corrected their position, balancing effortlessly on my hip. Other infants whimpered when their mother left the room or beamed with delight at her return. Sam seemed oblivious to my presence and was content whether I was there or not. When I approached, he failed to smile or acknowledge me until I spoke. As I talked, cooed and mimicked he would vocalise and chatter, enjoying our conversation.

At home, I felt a huge sense of responsibility. While Tim was at work it was down to me to make sure I did all the therapies, techniques and appointments. Tim is determined, hardworking and incredibly dedicated. I took to trying to care for Sam in a way I felt he would have done if he'd been at home. A warped sense of Tim and myself, combined with a sense of owing Sam my best, created a vat of expectations that burdened me daily.

I knew talking to Sammy was key and yet some days my emotions were so raw and dry this was a struggle. I would jolt myself as I realised I had been with Sam for the last hour and not uttered a word, simply locked in my own thoughts. That may sound strange, but when you have so very little feedback it becomes really hard to stay motivated and keep talking. I employed the use of the radio and television to fill Sam's world with stimulating voices and music.

Then I began dreading appointments. It wasn't that I feared the therapy or therapists but I feared what they saw in Sam. At the end of a visual impairment appointment, I would be encouraged to do fifteen minutes of visual stimulation each day. Then the occupational therapist would suggest just ten to twenty minutes of hand movements or actions. The speech and language therapist would give suggestions about communication and feeding. Then the physiotherapist would chip in with a thirty minute session of movements and stretches. I soon became sick and tired of it all.

Instead of a shopping basket of daily tasks, I found myself walking around with a shopping trolley of duties. Each time I encountered trained professionals they surreptitiously burdened me with more tasks and therapies. Daily I came to the checkout laden with duties and care that my energy and emotions couldn't afford.

When my friends moaned about the hassle of getting their baby out in the morning, I fought to hold my tongue. They appeared to live in another world and although they each had their own problems, I struggled with constantly wanting to explain the difficulties I faced. None of us were living in a perfect world. Some friends were living in abusive relationships, others suffered badly with postnatal depression, while I knew many women who would sorely love to hold a baby of their own and couldn't become pregnant. It wasn't that I thought my problems were bigger or more important, but some conversations highlighted problems I wish I could complain about.

"It's a nightmare; he's into everything."

"I just can't keep up with her; she does something new every day."

Enthusiastic and innocent comments struck a painful cord and made it harder for me to be around 'normal' babies and have 'normal' conversations.

On what must have been a particularly good day for me, Sam and I went out to buy some vegetables. I talked incessantly, playing the creative mother, while Sam took on the role of adoring son. As we neared the greengrocers I decided to be an über-mum and use the experience as a multi-sensory opportunity. We entered the open fronted shop and collected a basket.

"Here you go Sam feel this, it's an orange," I cooed, as I gently lifted Sam's hand the way the visual impairment specialist had shown me.

"Can you smell it?" I enquired.

"Clearly not Mum as its still got the skin on."

Okay, Sam didn't say that, but sometimes I wonder whether his silent half of the conversation is quite different to the one I'm imagining.

"And here Sam, this is a prickly, spiky pineapple. Wow, isn't it rough?" I chirped with perfect intonation and expression.

In recent months I had become used to staring strangers, however, I was so engrossed in trying to find as many adjectives to describe fruits that I failed to notice the gazing eye of the shopkeeper.

I was merrily talking away, answering my own questions, letting Sam touch and smell the fruit, when out of nowhere the shop assistant was standing next to me. I spun round and stood up, half expecting him to tell me off for fondling his fruit. As I looked into the shopkeeper's face he appeared stricken with a deep sense of both sympathy and confusion.

"Oh, er… I hope you don't mind, I'm just letting him feel and smell the fruit."

"Yes, of course," he replied, still looking slightly confused.

"You see his eyes don't work very well, so I, erm... well it's good for him to experience his environment with his other senses."

"Ah, yes, yes of course." His eyes lightened as though he had just had a revelation.

I bent down again and returned to my conversation with Sam, feeling rather smug. I had enlightened another layperson into the world of disability.

"You really should take him to see a doctor."

"Excuse me?" was all I could muster, as I stood to attention once more.

"I think you should take him to the doctors. See if there is anything they could do," he repeated.

"Er... well... yes," I stammered. He obviously believed his words of wisdom were sufficient and started heading back to the till, disinterested in anything else I may have to say. He seemed proud in his exemplary customer service of not only providing fresh varieties of fruit and vegetables, but medical advice too.

Sam and I quickly finished our feeling and smelling session, hurriedly paid for our produce and with a polite smile headed home. At times like this you make a decision to laugh or cry. That day I laughed. The idea that I had been sitting at home deciding my son was probably blind enough to touch fruit yet failed to seek medical advice was ridiculous.

Some conversations ended less well.

A few months later, I was feeling a little emotional and walking down an aisle in the supermarket. Sam was temporarily sporting a nasogastric tube coming out of his nose (you'll find out about it in more detail later). As a result he looked sick and mid browsing I spotted a middle-aged man staring at us. He was staring intensely with sad, sympathetic eyes and mouth wide open. I kept my head down and tried to avoid eye contact with the occasional smile to allay his concern. We continued walking as the gentleman headed towards us.

"Awww! Hello," he said.

"Hello." I smiled. "Sammy, say hello to the kind gentleman." I bent down touched Sam's hand, gave eye contact to the stranger and attempted to keep walking.

"What's the matter with him?" he asked, pointing vaguely towards Sam's face.

"You mean the tube? Well he can't swallow very well so he has that tube to help us feed him straight into his stomach."

"Aw, well I'm sure it will get better."

"Erm… No, I don't think it will," I mumbled. With hindsight and practice I know I should have smiled and walked away.

"Oh, you never know. Medical science is amazing these days. I'm sure it will all work out just fine."

"Yes, quite, but this is a chronic condition that isn't going to get fixed." My heart began to race at feeling the need to explain my son's prognosis to this stranger.

"Oh, I'm sure that isn't the case. There are all sorts of things they can do and if not now, I'm sure it will be just round the corner. You'll see."

Thoughts and words galloped from my mouth before I'd even taken a breath.

"Look, the reason he can't eat is because he has brain damage - extensive, complicated brain damage." Having raised my voice slightly, others in the aisle lifted their heads to look our way. "Permanent brain damage. And one of the many parts totally mushed is the bit that controls the very complex skill of swallowing. It isn't going to get better and there isn't anything

84

the doctors can do. In fact, he is waiting to have a permanent hole in his stomach for a tube, so that people don't stop me in supermarkets and try to give me medical advice about what I can expect in my son's future."

Another terse smile and I walked off, my lip quivering as tears tripped my cheeks. I dropped my basket at the entrance and left.

I know the stranger was only trying to be kind and positive, but I was so angry at feeling forced into contradicting his unfounded positive remarks. It is common for people to feel the need to be optimistic about Sam and his condition. It's as though they feel too awkward when it isn't ok. In some conversations I end up being more negative than necessary because the person I'm talking to doesn't ask open questions like, 'How's Sam doing?' or 'How are things?'

Rather, they begin with, 'Sam looks so much better. Is he doing really well?'

The question indicates the desire for good news. Inevitably, they get a cautious and more negative answer. Sometimes I make platitudes and go along with the game, but if I'm feeling grumpy or misunderstood, they may just get an abrupt response. The atmosphere of a conversation is dependent upon two major factors: whether a person wants to make Sam's condition rose tinted, and my own mental health.

I believe an honest and positive conversation requires both parties not dictating the answers and recognising we both face our own battles. A conversation isn't good because someone comes up with a solution or positive perspective; rather it's successful when both parties have been heard.

It takes true skill to simply listen, validating another person's feelings and viewpoint: I think it is a skill definitely worth perfecting.

12

It's Not the Same

"You have not walked in my footsteps, danced in my shoes, or lived in my world. Do not judge me, point your fingers at me, or become experts on my life. Instead, celebrate with me in times of joy and cry with me in times of pain. Only then will we begin to understand each other."

Kate Baker

I celebrated my first Mother's Day with a surprise spa day from Tim, while for Father's Day he got a T-shirt with a picture of Sam grinning on the front and 'I'm the daddy' on the back.

I think I got the better deal.

Sam had developed a real passion for music, becoming animated at songs he recognised, vocalising and making noises. Like Fred Astaire and Ginger Rogers, we sang and danced with eloquence and frivolity. He also began to show knowledge and pleasure about his routine. Sam appeared physically excited, when, after dinner, he was taken upstairs. We would lay him down in a shallow bath and he would kick, splash and smile. We soaked up these simple, enjoyable times doing normal things with our boy.

After bath time I dried Sam, dressed him and zipped him into his yellow giraffe sleeping bag. Then lying on his back he watched lights flashing above his cot whilst listening to a soothing baby CD. I would then run around putting laundry away and tidying the bathroom before settling down for a bedtime story.

I loved resting in the nursery chair as I held my warm bundle, with his delicious clean baby smell. We would read together and Sam would listen, kind of. He didn't look at the pictures nor point at any of the objects on the pages. Instead, I made my voice sound as much like a children's TV presenter as I could bear. Then, with the lights dimmed, I held my son in the silence at the end of a busy day. He rested in my arms for his night time feed, as his little body slowly relaxed into mine and gently dozed off to sleep.

Amidst the growing number of appointments and therapies, I tried to maintain some friendships outside the disabled world. I continued to meet with girls from my antenatal group and joined Claire with my nephew Josh for baby swimming lessons.

I enjoyed these times, although to do so required a perpetual state of being on-guard. I hadn't realised how exhausting it is trying to not be emotional. However, situations continued to hit me unexpectedly. At times, I was struck by the tragedy of Sam's disability in a new and more painful way.

I found myself becoming angry at comparisons between my experience of motherhood and those around me. If I was talking about a particularly stressful experience, the worst thing someone could say was 'it's just the same when I...' My reactive anger would erupt. I wanted to know people understood what I was going through. Yet as my friends and family spoke of similarities, the canyon of differences only became clearer. As I sat on my little island of motherhood, some people simply couldn't see me; they thought my island was a close replica of their own.

But it wasn't the same.

I found it tiring having conversations with mums comparing struggles and issues. So I spent more time with friends who could listen, without giving a quick fix or comparison in return.

One such person was Alex. She is the kind of super-woman I aspire to be. She's thoughtful, loyal, and has a capacity to love and forgive greater than anyone else I know. Her ability to see me on my island has been second to none. Our friendship was forged on walking alongside each other, sharing, listening and not necessarily trying to fix what we faced.

When Sam was about six months old, my mum was coming over from Buckingham regularly to help while I continued my work as a nurse at a local GP surgery. One morning in spring, both my parents came to visit. I sat on the bed in my pyjamas while Sam lay on top of the ruffled duvet. Suddenly the conversation turned serious.

"We want to talk to you about something," Mum said glancing at Dad, indicating he was to take it from here. In return, he smiled in recognition of my mum's age-old trick and began to describe their heart to share our burden. They wanted to move closer, to help look after Sam and be part of his future. Their words and commitment demonstrated they could see our island, its differences and struggles. Not only could they see it, they offered to live there too. It was a most powerful expression of support for our little family. When I later discussed their proposal with Tim, he wasn't even slightly deterred by the prospect of his mother-in-law moving to town. We enthusiastically agreed and Mum and Dad started making plans to move to Southend a year later in the summer of 2007.

My parents are, however, unique. Understandably, the majority of people struggle to comprehend what life is like parenting a child with a complex disability. It's like trying to explain to someone who doesn't have children what being a parent is like. It is possible to explain the emotions, detail the grief, outline the practical difficulties, and paint a picture of the challenging future but no description of the parts accurately portrays the sum of them.

In the same way, a landscape painting is nothing compared to standing in the same beautiful valley; watching the clouds shift, feeling the wind through your hair and hearing the unique seasonal birdsong.

It quite simply is not the same.

It isn't possible to fully articulate the experience of being in love, to someone who has yet to fall in love. Nor can you explain what it feels like to be a parent. Similarly, I can't explain what it's like to be the mum of a beautiful little boy like Sam. Each of these things are not logical or intellectual, they are deeper and richer. They come into that untold, unexplained part of life that defines the reason we live and enjoy living. Call it magical or spiritual; it is irrational, human, powerful and unique.

Sadly, my failure to realise this truth left me feeling wronged and angered by people who apparently didn't get it. I felt trapped by the facade of coping and rarely feeling that people around me understood what I was going through. Mostly I enjoyed play dates with friends, but then on other days everything seemed harder. Every baby appeared so much more engaging and everywhere I looked, I was reminded of what Sam couldn't do.

One day, Tim gave me the morning off and I sat on Two Tree Island thinking, crying and reflecting on life. On a scrappy piece of paper I wrote:

It isn't the same
My son isn't like yours
He isn't the same
My world isn't like yours
We're not the same
You have hard times and struggles
But they aren't the same
My world
My life
They aren't the same
My future, my experiences
They aren't the same
How you look at me
Isn't the same
How we look at country paths, bicycles,
Trampolines and beaches
Isn't the same
You see opportunities, I see hurdles
It isn't the same.

I struggled having no idea how to anticipate or predict our future. When we went back to the Hammersmith Hospital in early June, we hoped to add a pencil sketch to the picture of our future.

We sat in the cramped waiting area jammed with chairs, kids, toys and a large hospital games console. We drove rather than taking the train, having learnt the lessons of earlier appointments. The fish tank in the corner hummed quietly, presumably intending to have a calming effect on the waiting children.

I began to look at those around me; babies with tubes in their nose, infants sitting limp and dribbling. Older children were strapped into big cumbersome wheelchairs. I lovingly looked at Sam and couldn't imagine him aged three, six or thirteen. I knew his little brain was damaged enough to make his skull small and slightly misshapen, but he didn't even need medication.

His soft, squidgy body appeared perfect. I wondered if I could love him with the same passion if he had thin, twisted, lifeless limbs. Sam lay silently sleeping in his pushchair, oblivious to his environment and my thoughts.

"Samuel Wright." The words echoed down the corridor.

Doctor Cowen shook our hands and indicated where we should sit. She introduced us to a couple of junior doctors before the questions began. Gaps in the information from Southend Hospital occurred, as tests hadn't been taken or communicated. We told them about Sam's occasional blank spells and that he would sit unsupported for only a very short period of time. He was allergic to milk, but he was weaning quite well. His poor vision meant he didn't see the food coming and he hadn't developed any preferences, but he was eating small amounts of my puréed, home cooked grub.

Doctor Cowen listened, smiled, nodded and took notes as we spoke. She confirmed his development was progressing in line with his MRI. She was hopeful he wouldn't have any problems with feeding and that he would eventually sit unaided. Although he was unlikely to ever walk with any function, he may one day take a step. Her words hit like a gale force wind, unsteadying my feet. It wasn't easy but at least we had a sketch, some clarity to our future. Our life would have wheelchairs and disabled equipment.

She was most concerned about Sam's vision and its lack of progress. Overall, the doctors seemed pleased with Sam, although I felt I had lost a little more hope. I was glad to have

91

some clear expectations, no matter how hard they were to hear.

We discussed what had actually happened to Sam, and whether it would happen again. All the metabolic and thrombophilic screens were negative. It remained unclear, but the best guess was that an infection or incident assaulted Sam's brain in the couple of days before his birth, complicated further by resuscitation at delivery. There was no evidence to suggest it would happen again.

On our way home we talked about having another baby. Our discussion boiled down to some simple truths. Sam was only going to get harder to look after. There was no point in us waiting for him to toilet train, walk or feed himself. So the decision was made to be more relaxed about not not getting pregnant.

14

Tim's Story

Doctor v Dad: 18th July 2006

"Appreciate what you have, before time teaches you to appreciate what you had."

Unknown

Tim's pager's piercing bleep sliced through the air, like a wailing baby demanding immediate care. The humdrum chatter of the canteen failed to dampen its call for attention. Plates clattered and cutlery chinked while men and women began rummaging around. Startled and dismayed eyes darted about, like a flock of ducks once distracted by mouldy bread but now frightened by the unwanted barking of a dog. Hands searched for the offending pager.

Tim joined the gaggle, putting down his fork and glancing at his hip.

"It's mine," he confirmed, barely looking up.

A collective sigh of relief emanated as eating the indistinguishable hospital canteen lunch resumed, while Tim screeched back his chair to stand.

The pager's sound instantly incurred a heart-sinking feeling in his chest. No sacred time or place was protected from its penetrating noise, indicating someone else was petitioning for time and energy.

"Hi, it's Tim, you bleeped me?"

Propping the canteen phone between his ear and shoulder he removed a scrappy piece of paper, adding another task with a scrawl more indecipherable by the hour.

"Ok, I've got a couple of other things to do first. I will try to be there before two," he confirmed.

Tim hung up the receiver and accepted lunch was over. Leaving the canteen, he paused in the stairwell to call me.

"Hello?"

"Hi, I just had my lunch. It's really busy but I thought I'd call and see how you both are."

"I'm not sure really." I hesitated.

"Why? What's the matter?"

"At physio this morning Sam did some little twitches. Like small electric shocks, his arms jerked out and his fingers flared."

"What did Rosemary say?"

"She pointed it out. Once she mentioned it, I noticed a few. She suggested we take him to see a doctor."

"How is he now? Does he have a temperature?"

"I don't know I haven't checked. Well... actually yes, he does feel a bit hot. It is warm today though."

"Maybe give him some paracetamol and see how he goes. Call me if you're worried otherwise I'll see him as soon as I get home."

"Ok."

"Love you, and I'll call later if I can."

"Ok, I'll let you go, bye."

Tim's mind raced with all the possible explanations for Sam's twitching, as a funnel of concern drained into a growing well of anxiety. Once the call ended, he made the switch from husband to doctor, like being snapped from hypnosis he was flung from one world to another. The incessant demands of the hospital and looming to-do list prevented any further dissection of the facts, as the shrill of his pager was greeted with a sigh.

An hour passed and while signing off drug charts Tim's phone vibrated enthusiastically in his pocket with my call. Retreating from the desk, he snuck into a side room to answer.

"Hello, is everything ok?"

"No, not really." I answered, "I'm in the supermarket and Sam is sitting in the trolley's baby seat, and he's twitching *a lot*."

"What do you mean?" Tim's voice echoed with concern.

"It isn't so much his body, although that's jerking a little, it's his face. It gets all contorted like he's having funny little spasms. I don't know what to do."

"Why are you shopping?" The question sounded sharper than intended.

"Well, once I had taken off some of his layers Sammy cooled down and seemed fine. So, I popped in to get dinner on the way home. He's just done another one. I'm really worried Tim. I don't know what it is or what I should do?"

"Has he had any paracetamol?"

"No, not yet."

"Give him a dose as soon as you can and get home. Call me and let me know how he is."

"Ok, I'm sorry if I did the wrong thing."

"Don't worry. Just get him home and tell me how it goes."

"Ok, bye."

Exhaling under the added burden of knowledge and responsibility, Tim breathed deeply before continuing his duties at the hospital while his heart and head longed to be home. He remained focused on ensuring the seemingly endless tasks didn't delay his home time at nine o'clock.

In the dimming light of the warm July evening Tim finally stepped out of the hospital and searched for his mobile. All the things he had done that day caused his head to swim, and his thoughts were laced with the fear that an important chore was omitted or poor decision made. He began to walk home, and with each step away from the hospital, he consciously allowed his shoulders to relax.

He pressed fast dial.

"Hi, I'm on my way. How's Sam? You were going to call me."

"Sorry, I got side tracked. He had some paracetamol, ate his dinner fine, enjoyed a playful bath-time and went to bed well. He even took a decent amount of milk. I've checked on him a couple of times and he's really settled."

"That's a relief."

"Sorry I didn't call, I've been running around getting the house straight for you coming in, hoping that we could have a nice dinner together."

"That sounds lovely. I'm on my way and won't be long."

Once home Tim kicked off his shoes in the hallway, slid his workbag under the shelf by the front door and used the white gloss bannister as a coat hook before beginning up the stairs.

"Dinner's ready if you want to come through?" I injected trying to usher him into the dining room.

"No, I want to see Sam. I've been thinking about him all day."

The terraced house stairs creaked as our conversation continued up to Sam's bedroom. Quietly Tim opened the door, fearful not to wake Sam unnecessarily. I followed just a couple

96

of steps behind.

"Rachel, Sam's fitting!" Tim stammered into the dark warm air.

"What?"

Frantically, Tim yanked the dimmer switch to full strength, as its brightness revealed the horrifying truth of the situation.

"Oh my goodness. Tim, I'm sorry. I'm so sorry. I should've had the monitor on but I didn't. I checked on him less than half an hour ago, I promise."

As Tim tenderly lifted Sam's writhing, flinching body he looked me in the eyes. "Rachel, call an ambulance."

Feeling helpless and as though in slow motion Tim gently unwrapped Sam from his yellow giraffe sleeping bag and stripped him to his vest.

"It's ok Sammy, Daddy's here. It's ok. We'll get you to the hospital."

Gently smoothing his hot head he grabbed the thermometer on the chest of drawers and was shocked to see it reach forty degrees without effort. Fighting back fears and frustration at not being able to treat his own son, he offered low, soft words of reassurance. In the background he heard my guilt strained voice as I shakily asked for an ambulance, gave our address and explained the situation.

Tim looked up as I stepped back into the nursery and slunk next to him on the floor. Sam's little body heaved and jolted between us while his face contorted and grimaced over and over. Looking into Tim's eyes, my emotions bubbled over with welling tears.

"I'm so sorry," I pleaded, "I'm so sorry."

"I know. You pack a bag for the hospital and I'll go downstairs and wait for the ambulance."

Tim opened the front door and turned on all the lights and wasn't waiting in the living room long before an ambulance man walked in.

"Hi, there. How are you doing?" He smiled.

"Not great. I've just come home from work, checked on my son and he's fitting."

"Has he fitted before?" enquired the driver reaching down to his bag of tricks.

"No, this is the first time, but he has cerebral palsy and a very high temperature."

"Ok, it's probably a febrile convulsion. I'll get some oxygen from the car."

"Do you have any rectal diazepam or anything to stop the seizure?"

"Ideally those drugs are given at the hospital, especially if he hasn't had them before."

"He might have been fitting for over half an hour. Can we just go straight to A&E?" asserted Tim.

"Well, let me just get some oxygen and see if that helps."

"How exactly is that going to help? He has a fever of over forty, we don't have any rectal paracetamol to treat his temperature and he needs medication to stop his seizure. Let's just get in the ambulance and go."

The uncharacteristic firmness of Tim's tone surprised everyone in the room.

Another ambulance crew member walked in and it became clear the first man to arrive had come in a car. Paperwork was taken out of a bag.

"What's your son's name?"

"Samuel Wright, but let's talk on the way to resus. You can't treat him and he may already be in status. He needs to be seen now."

Tim got up and walked towards the door, sidestepping the ambulance man. His pen stopped mid writing as the ambulance staff looked at each other quizzically.

"Look. I'm a doctor at the hospital. It's been a long day and I know there is nothing any of us can do here. We have packed a bag, let's go now and you can tell resus we're on our way."

The ambulance men glanced at each other as another female crew member walked in and smiled at everyone.

"I've just had to leave the ambulance in the middle of the road. The double parking on these streets is a nightmare," she quipped against the tense atmosphere.

"Well you won't be parked long," Tim challenged, as he carried Sam through the front door and waited on the pavement seething with frustration. The same cocktail of feelings emanating from knowledge and helplessness flooded his mind, triggering a flashback of watching Sam being resuscitated at birth.

Within minutes of reaching home, Tim was heading back to the hospital void of a to-do list but a greater burden than any task undertaken all day. We talked breezily about what to expect next and how to manage the practicalities of calling family and friends.

The ambulance hurtled into the emergency bay outside A&E's resus as a doctor and nurse stood waiting by the gaping double doors. We had both stood in the exact same spot waiting to receive the casualties of a car crash. No physical scrapes or scars were visible on our family, but it felt as though we had suffered a horrific pile-up.

In resus, the medics and nurses frantically tried to get access to Sam's veins as each new attempt to stop the seizure failed. We hoped our gentle words and soothing touches offered a balm to Sam's writhing body amidst the bleeps and bustle of the hospital.

Minutes eked by as nearly an hour of watching occurred before our baby's body stopped shaking and squirming. Finally, he relaxed and his breathing became calm and deep.

By eleven o'clock Tim lay awake, as I gently snored beside him. He gazed across the small side room, lit with the green glare of a rising and falling line from the cardiac monitor. He watched our son, sound asleep. Having dissected the day's events his mind continued to buzz with future possibilities.

The alien landscape we had lived in over the last nine months had dared to become familiar. Watching shapes pass the room's frosted window, Tim held me silently in the shadows knowing that once again the terrain of our lives had changed.

15

Seizures

"When you've been broken, broken to pieces.
And Your heart begins to faint, 'cause you don't understand."
Kevin Prosch

The morning after the seizure Sam appeared back to normal. I watched him lie in his hospital cot smiling and cooing, oblivious to the disturbing memories acquired the night before. It appeared he had avoided any long-term effects. I sighed with relief as though having dropped something, only to realise it wasn't irretrievably broken.

Given that Sam hadn't shown any signs of fitting prior to being unwell, the doctors were optimistic that he had simply suffered a common febrile convulsion. Therefore, Sam was discharged without starting epilepsy medication. However, I was much more jumpy about any sound he made and the monitor was *always* on. I was also grateful for my engaging, sociable and fun little boy.

Just a couple of weeks after Sam's first seizure I stood next to Tim in our 1980s grey tiled bathroom whispering. Sam was asleep in his room across the corridor but that wasn't why we were being quiet.

"You look," I urged.

"Is it time yet?"

"I think so."

Once again, Tim was holding a piece of plastic I had recently peed on. This time his dimples were buried beneath the pale look of trepidation. His expression indicated both our feelings.

We were pregnant.

Sam was nine months old and had begun to show glimpses of his true colours. Yet now I had another little being growing inside of me. Although it wasn't an accident and we were pleased, we were also daunted at opening ourselves up again to the potential joy and pain of pregnancy and birth.

My response to this critically emotional time was to promptly start vomiting everywhere again and in this instance, practice did not make perfect. I continued to hate being sick as I knelt on the bathroom floor, longing for someone to hold back my hair and wipe my brow.

When Sam was ten months old we were visiting my parents in Buckingham, when Sam spiked another temperature. As before, he began twitching and jolting; our anxiety growing with every temperature related jerk.

"Look that was another one," I exclaimed, as we crouched on the bed over our hot and poorly baby.

"I know. They are getting more frequent."

"What do you think we should do?"

"Well if he starts fitting here we're about twenty minutes from A&E. Maybe we should just get in the car and go now.'

"Ok, I'll pack the bag and tell my parents. You get Sam in his car seat."

After a short time in A&E, Sam was admitted to the paediatric ward for observation.

102

The next morning I woke on a large reclining chair feeling achy and crotchety. I stared at Sam lying peacefully in his metal-framed cot with a heavily bandaged arm protecting the needle in his vein. Later that morning, Sam began to spike another temperature and the twitching returned with a vengeance. I called a doctor over to witness the jerks I had described and in front of our eyes, my son started fitting again.

"Diazepam please," shouted the doctor, as she hit the alarm. Medical staff started running around, yet even with medication straight into the vein the fit still lasted more than twenty minutes.

A couple of days later we were back in Southend discussing these events with Sam's consultant. An urgent EEG was arranged (where lots of electrodes are stuck to Sam's scalp to read the electrical impulses of his brain). I took Sam home after the EEG but he continued to be unwell and have high temperatures. By the time Tim came back from work that evening (as a doctor on the same paediatric ward) Sam looked so weak that we returned to his colleagues with a mottled, limp and hot little boy. Immediately, antibiotics and fluids were prescribed and while we stood in the little, dim side room the consultant came in to discuss Sam's EEG results.

He immediately grinned and greeted Tim with a shake of his hand.

"Hi Tim. How are you?"

"Not so great." He shrugged, nodding towards his sick son lying in the cot.

"Mmmm ... yes. Well the EEG shows some marked accelerations. As well as background activity, there are definitive spikes and seizural changes. So I've told the nurses to draw up some sodium valporate. Over the next few weeks you will need to titrate it up to reach a maintenance dose." He hesitated, looking over at Sam and smiling.

"Anyway I'll leave you to it," he quipped with a nod. "Do call me if you need anything, alright?"

"Yes, okay, thanks." Tim smiled and walked over to Sam. Bending down, he picked up his soft hand as the doctor left the room.

"What did he just say? What does that mean?" I asked.

"He just told me my son has epilepsy."

Tim's eyes showed the heartbreak of a father, while his colleagues were treating him like a doctor. He hugged me like a husband and kissed Sam's head like a dad. Epilepsy medications were started and gradually increased in the hope they would stem any further seizures.

Then soon after Sam turned one, and I was four months pregnant, the fitting nightmare worsened. Tim and I had just returned from a short trip to Geneva, while my parents cared for Sam. We spent a night with friends in south London because Katie had kindly offered to drive us to an appointment at Great Ormond Street Hospital. We were driving along the Thames, past Vauxhall Bridge, when Sam did a twitch whilst sleeping in his car seat.

"Tim, Sam's just jerked," I choked from my seat next to Sam, as anxiety rose in my voice.

"What do you mean jerked?" Tim looked around from the front passenger seat.

"He's just had a twitch." I looked up and saw fear reflected in my husband's eyes.

"Is he hot?"

"It's hard to tell he's so tightly strapped in his car seat." I responded in frustration.

"Pass me some paracetamol from his bag and I'll give it to him," I instructed.

As Tim rummaged through Sam's baby bag, the twitches and jerks grew closer together, like the narrowing contractions of a pregnant woman. We passed Lambeth Bridge when the seizure started unfolding. Katie fought back panic and drove us the two hundred metres to St. Thomas's A&E and stopped across an ambulance bay.

Immediately, someone came out to complain about our choice of parking but as soon as they saw Tim holding a fitting Sam they swung the doors open and directed him towards the paediatric resuscitation area. Doctors once again began futile attempts to get Sam out of his fit. On this occasion, Sam required sedation and ventilation before being transferred to the paediatric intensive care unit.

In many ways this fit was even harder to handle. I discovered it doesn't become easier seeing your son fight for his life. This well-worn path wasn't any less difficult to tread. The horror of seeing the doctors scrabble around, as each new medical technique failed, didn't wane. The aftermath felt all the more harrowing because of the contrast from the previous week. Any rest and refreshment we had acquired in Switzerland vanished. Our relaxing holiday and warm bubble baths had been swapped for the stale, traumatic atmosphere of the intensive care unit.

Over the following months, a pattern began to emerge. Whenever Sam developed a mild childhood illness, he would spike a temperature that set him on course for a life threatening fit.

When we returned to the Hammersmith Hospital with Sam, aged one year, the news wasn't good. Six months earlier the doctor's words and predictions had been hard to swallow, yet now, even they seemed optimistic.

Sam was struggling to feed, he was no longer able to sit

without lots of support, and suddenly the doctors were talking about palliative care. The severity of Sam's fits meant he was likely to die in childhood.

When the report letter from the appointment arrived, it landed with a thud on the doormat. Its words reverberated in my head and for days I felt shaken to the core. Doctor Cowen summed things up beautifully when she wrote,

'I was hopeful when I saw Sam last... but that was not the case today. I had been more optimistic... but I now think this [walking, sitting etc.] is unlikely. Samuel will have significant cognitive difficulties but it is pleasing that he is such a nice, happy and smiling boy who certainly responds to his parents.'

Once again, Sam was on the wrong end of the statistics. Any optimism expressed by medical staff had been unfounded. With time, I was able to appreciate the blessing that was Sam engaging and responding to us, although it didn't gloss over the pain.

In the coming years, the impact of Sam's seizures grew. Every journey was planned knowing I may need to call an ambulance, and when Sam wasn't with me, my phone never left my side. For months and years, I walked around with every muscle in my body tense; braced for the next time the world stood still while my son writhed.

*

When Sam was three he changed the rules again and the epilepsy tightrope became even more perilous. Day by day my feet sought out the wire beneath them fearing the slightest wobble would send us over the edge into the ravine below. We started phoning for an ambulance every two to three weeks, calling the crew members by name. On two occasions Tim was required to give Sam mouth-to-mouth resuscitation to keep him alive during a fit.

I clearly remember crawling into bed early one night feeling physically and emotionally exhausted. I lay and wept. Living had become relentless and unpredictable, so in exhaustion I cried out, "I can't do this anymore. It is too hard. I'm too tired. I'm too stretched. I'm at my limit. Enough is enough."

I drifted off to sleep with a tear stained face. Forty minutes later, a sinister sound crept through the baby monitor. What could have been innocent gurgling sounded insidious to my rousing consciousness. Fear crept up my spine like cold ice tentacles, forcing my lifeless body to jump out of bed and race into Sam's room.

"Tim! Sam's fitting," I screamed down the stairs as tears retraced their path down my cheeks, in part for my son's writhing body, but also for my own insipid spirit. I had become a hollow reflection of myself, simply existing moment to moment.

Sitting by Sam's cot in hospital, expletives rose to my lips as I received a text from a good friend.

'2 Corinthians 4 verse 18' it simply read. I looked up the verse.

'So we fix our eyes not on what is seen, but on what is unseen, since what is seen is temporary but what is unseen is eternal.'

I was incredulous. I felt crushed, squashed and manipulated by what was seen; whether I liked it or not. How could I live any other way?

That night I lay on the same single bed I had with Tim the night after Sam's first fit as the glow of the monitor once again lit the room. While muffled footsteps passed in the corridor I realised I *had* to fix my eyes on what was *unseen*. What I saw around me was unpredictable and frightening.

People had glibly suggested I needed to trust God, rely on him, and live without fear. They implied that God would make it all okay and I had no need to worry. I thought it was responsible to fear Sam's fits and their impact. If we hadn't been so diligent and responsive, there would have been many occasions where Sam could have died. It is right to fear being knocked over by a car because it makes you careful when crossing the road. Yet I had to work out how I could fear something terrible and likely, without living my life *in* fear.

My faith had to transcend what was happening in my life. It couldn't be dependent on my experience or on a belief that I would be sheltered from tough times. If it had done, my faith, like my emotions, would have ended in tatters. Although it had been suggested to me that 'everything happens for a reason,' I finally let myself off the hook of finding reason or an unfathomable purpose in my son's pain. I let go of the image of God playing chess with his life, deciding how or when to teach me a lesson through Sam's struggles. Instead, I allowed myself to simply live with the grief and choose love.

There was so much I couldn't change. So much of the 'seen' world was out of my control, yet I came to realise that I still had decisions to make. In that dark place, I could choose anger, fear, bitterness and resentment, or something else. Sam had little choice and yet I could clearly see goodness oozing out of him. He continued to bring the best out in people and filled the world around him with smiles and love. Ultimately, I believed in a good God, even when so much around me was bad.

No amount of positives made my experience acceptable though. It didn't put a gloss on it. A bad thing is still bad, but I decided out of it I could either sow seeds that destroyed me or seeds with the potential to bear fruit. It was easy to see ways I could be changed for the positive. It was harder to watch Sam suffer with no benefit in sight, leaving me with the question, why wouldn't God just take it all away? On some days, simply trusting that there was a greater power holding my world together felt like a big leap of faith.

*

Around Sam's fourth birthday his medications were changed and his serious fits stabilised. Years have passed without calling an ambulance or administering midazolam. My shoulders rest well below my ears but I am forever on guard. I know at any time I may be required to walk the epilepsy tightrope again and each day I carry secret scars; wounds inflicted by memories of watching Sam shake, writhe and fail to breathe.

Today I anticipate the next time, when an older Sam will fit in a new place and in different circumstances, but the grimacing and writhing will be the same. My emotions will flood with familiar memories of watching my son fit. Like scratching my eczema and causing it to bleed, witnessing another seizure will break my fragile, partially healed heart. Then I will be left broken and exposed, wondering if this seizure will suck Sam's last breath: Will this be how Sam dies?

16

Feeding

"Tell me what you eat, and I will tell you what you are."
Anthelme Brillat-Savarin

Initially Sam appeared to feed well. I was surprised to find that I actually enjoyed breastfeeding and it had the added bonus of justifying me eating extra calories. I gorged myself with cakes and biscuits in justifiable glee that I was simply taking on the nutrients needed to sustain my baby. The fact that I consistently overcompensated the amount of calories required is best overlooked. Feeding also made me sit down with Sam and just hold him, helping me soak up this little boy as we talked about what we had done and how much I loved him, or we'd simply flick on the TV and watch Loose Women together.

Once the early pain had subsided, breastfeeding was relatively easy and I had a reputation of being able to pump an excessive amount of milk. Amongst friends I was deemed the breastfeeding super hero of the Noughties. I went from my teenage 'A' cup to practically signing a contract with Tesco, as one of their named dairies, in under a year. I could just see a smiling photo of me on the side of a milk carton with 'Rachel, from Essex' written alongside.

When it was time to start weaning I bought the book

everyone was talking about and started making my own wholesome Annabel Karmel baby delights. I would fill my kitchen with pots, pans and a host of freshly bought veg (from our lovely, overly helpful, local greengrocer). Unfortunately, Sam wasn't easy to feed. He didn't appear to like the taste of anything in particular, leaving me spending ages getting a few mouthfuls into him. Everything had to be puréed, as even the tiniest lump would cause him to choke and vomit.

One evening I cleaned Sam's mouth as he sat in his highchair, and took a second look. As I wiped away a slop of red foodstuff, I became worried it had stained his face. I stood back and wondered why he looked like he had a tan. I examined the dining room for anything orange that may be reflecting on him but found nothing. I began to worry he had developed jaundice.

"Tim," I called towards the front room, "can you come here please?" With a sigh I heard footsteps come our way.

"What's the matter?" asked Tim.

"Take a look at Sam."

"Yes?"

"Do you think he looks a bit... orange?"

Tim carried out a very detailed examination of his son and made a serious diagnosis. Sam had turned a faint orangey tone as a result of his zealous and determined mother feeding him too much red baby food.

I had created my own oompa-loompa.

With my attempts of supplying Sam with super foods, I had inadvertently served up a heavy dose of carotene (red colouring in vegetables like carrots and sweet potato). So much so, that I had made his skin turn slightly orange. Sam was now somewhere between being Tango'd and a Ready Brek baby. His diet was promptly changed to contain more 'green' and less

111

'red' but he remained difficult to feed. At about ten months of age, when Sam's fits were getting worse, his feeding deteriorated so much that I dared to face the nightmare that is the 'Baby Weigh-in Clinic'.

On the whole I found it best to avoid groups of 'normal' babies and health visitors; both caused me a headache and neither had anything sensible to say. Reluctantly, I padlocked the pushchair to the railings outside and joined the throng of women in the large, dull waiting area. Peeling paint and thinning, brown industrial carpet completed the enticing NHS look as we sat crammed together on our plastic chairs. I focused on Sam and kept my head down wanting to avoid the other mothers and their severe condition of 'over-shoulder-itis'.

Previously docile, pleasant women give birth and morph into competitive mothers committed to comparing their little darlings to everyone else the same age. Women either side of me sat chatting, finding subtle ways of injecting all the 'new' things their babies were doing into the conversation. I would daydream about mothers watching their infants play on the floor only to lift up a scorecard like a judge on *Strictly Come Dancing*.

"Seven!" one mum would declare.

"Four!" another would yell as the crowd jeered in disapproval of the harsh scoring.

The main attraction of the clinic however is the weigh-in and it's a whole different league to Weight Watchers. As we sat around, mild excitement would ripple the room as another mum exited gleefully muttering, "He's put on another pound."

The unabashed pride was akin to a mum whose baby had reached a developmental milestone two years early. Eventually, I discovered that if I arrived a few minutes before the end of the session, I could avoid the maze of pushchairs and chitchat. I

112

simply slipped in and out without talking to anyone except the health visitor - sadly, I couldn't avoid her.

My fears were confirmed. Although Sam still looked relatively chunky, his weight had plateaued and he was dropping his centiles. Before long, lunchtime was taking about an hour and his failure to feed was affecting his growth.

During one of Sam's admissions for a seizure it became obvious to everyone he wasn't eating enough. This resulted in a temporary nasogastric tube being inserted. It was agreed that we should start Sam on high calorie milk. After he had eaten orally, we would supplement his meal with milk via the tube stuck to his cheek.

My boy suddenly looked different.

My baby bag no longer held the usual nappies, wipes and feed, but also PH paper and syringes. My well-rehearsed nursing skills were superseding my maternal role, as previously separate worlds were merging.

On the day I left hospital with Sam and his tube, I walked the short distance from the hospital to Rachel's house. The stare count jumped several notches as people passed us making sympathetic nods of the head and quiet sighs. A lump grew in my throat as I allowed my eyes to follow the cracks in the pavement ahead. I reminded myself my boy hadn't changed. He was the same little boy and my love was no less real or sufficient.

As I began to process this, I dared to gaze up and narrowly missed bumping into three people staggering along the road coming in the opposite direction. They were each tightly gripping cans of super-strong cider. The young woman in the group vocalised what everyone else we had passed were thinking.

"Aaah! Look at that little baby. Is he alright love?"

113

"Kind of. That tube is just to help him feed as he isn't getting enough."

"Aaaaah... That's so sad. I hope he's alright, bless him."

I kept walking, desperate to find the safety of Rachel's. She opened the door and stepped back to allow us in. Looking down at Sam she exclaimed, "Oh, he does look quite sick now doesn't he?"

I swallowed hard and made a mental note not to go back to the greengrocer until I had enough emotional resolve to deal with the potential comments.

In the following months the stares continued. When Sam had taken all the feed he could orally, I drew back some gastric juices (vomit to you and me) with a syringe and squirted it on a PH strip to check the tube was in the correct position. Then after attaching another tube to an open-ended 60ml syringe, I would stand and pour down the milk. This was an inconvenience at home and a complete spectacle when out. If ever before I had enjoyed attention, I loathed it now.

Sam and I no longer blended into the crowd; we stood out like a sore thumb. On the few occasions I went out without Sam, the first thing I noticed was the anonymity. No one looked twice at me as I slipped through crowds of people unseen. With Sam and his tube, I now felt we were primarily identified by his disability.

17

Birthdays: 12th October 2006

"Our birthdays are feathers in the broad wing of time."
Jean Paul

I remember loving birthdays as a child. When travelling in Uganda the poignancy of thanking God for our friends' birth and the privilege of sharing our lives with them, was not lost on me. As we headed towards Sam's first birthday, I realised the day was more about marking an anniversary than celebrating a birth. I was incredibly grateful for my beautiful son but his birth marked the beginning of the toughest year of my life.

Unwittingly, I began the treacherous road of reliving the past inch by inch. There were few details that passed me by, as I tiptoed through the events leading up to Sam's birth. I took note of the day I finished work, with a healthy baby nestled within me. I thought of the last time I went for a swim and the journey home from my college course singing full volume in the car, the day before my due date.

Like replaying the rhythm and rhyme of a familiar sullen song, I drew Tim into a melody that failed to get easier to sing. In our conversations we swayed to well-rehearsed words, rehashing the decisions we had made and what we could have done differently. By the time I got to the night before Sam's birthday, I was weary from repeating the same song and reliving the same events.

Sitting in Sam's room, I watched his mobile make shadows on the wall, while my baby slept. Despite knowing my blessings, I wept bitterly with grief as the past year overwhelmed me. It was the depth of my love and devotion that heightened the pain and heartache. I felt wracked with guilt for failing to protect my son and then ashamed of the grief I experienced. I wept for the struggles my son would suffer and ached with a love that felt beyond me.

Finally, I was thankful. I was thankful for Sam.

Sam's birthday funnelled a year of emotions and experiences into a twenty-four hour period. It wasn't a death I was commemorating or grieving, but a life I loved and cherished. Yet along with the joy and blessings, came pain and trials. It wasn't an anniversary that I could grieve and move on from. Instead, each year brought me deeper into problems, pleasures and complications.

I didn't plan a birthday party for Sam. I bravely went to others' and celebrated with presents and party food. Liz kindly arranged a joint party for Arthur, Sam and Sophie. With balloons, party hats and music aplenty, we all enjoyed marking the fact that we had been mothers for a year.

The birthday photos depict three wonderful smiling babies, one with a tube hanging from his cheek. There are only three days between their birthdays. Julia, Sophie's mum, was the lady opposite me on the antenatal ward the day Sam was born. She too had come for reassurance because she couldn't feel her baby move. She too sat anxiously strapped to a monitor. Two days later Sophie was born following an induction, fit and well. Arthur arrived the day after that and the trio was complete. Three days separated the beginning of their lives. Three days can be a very long time.

As it turned out my grandma had suffered a fall, so on Sam's birthday we went to visit her in hospital. There we met my sister-in-law, Claire, with my niece and nephew, Charlotte and Josh.

We squeezed into Grandma's hospital side room and Sam was given his presents and cards before we shared the birthday cake. Charlotte gave a fantastic rendition of *Happy Birthday*; the kind only a beautiful three-year-old can give. Then, after kissing Grandma goodbye we headed back to the car for the journey home. I wept.

How had this happened?

How did it turn out so very differently for us?

The difference between Sam and Josh aged one was already very obvious; the contrast would only be heightened with each passing year as the similarities waned.

That evening Tim and I had dinner together and enjoyed holding and playing with Sam. Cosseted in our home our family felt perfect and we celebrated our little boy. By nighttime, I was thankful to crawl into bed, grateful the day was over. I was hopeful his second birthday would be an improvement.

I was wrong.

In an attempt to counteract the emotions and forthcoming dissection of events, I planned a swimming pool party on Sam's second birthday.

Sam loves swimming. When he hits the water, he instantly smiles and his whole body responds with delight. He kicks his legs, splashes his arms and laughs out loud. The swimming pool is an even field. Whether disabled or not, all of Sam's friends could join in the pleasure of the day.

Unfortunately, at 5am on Sam's second birthday we were

woken with that dreaded sound emanating from the baby monitor. Sam was fitting. So, instead of opening gifts together in bed, we called an ambulance and headed to A&E. This became a theme for the next three years as Sam was either in hospital or sick on his birthday.

As the years have passed, buying Sam presents has become more difficult. He has grown older but no more able and it's increasingly difficult to buy appropriate gifts: gifts that aren't babies' toys or clothes.

Buying presents for nieces and nephews is fun, although I'm not necessarily very timely with their delivery. Amazon even has a helpful button for 'Boy aged 6' to assist the shopping. The idea of buying Sam presents, however, makes Christmas and birthdays stressful. There isn't a 'Boy aged 4 who is blind, can't sit, doesn't talk and is unable to move arms or legs in a useful manner' option. If there were, I would have directed all of our relatives to it.

Birthdays give my imagination free rein to delve into holographic visions of what I expected life to be like. These images feel so strong and real, they are like memories, stolen from me, and I grieve them as such. In truth, they are mirages, figments of my imagination that never were and never would be.

Today, I try to handle this inevitability differently by recognising the loss I feel, expressing it, weeping and trying to ground it in reality. If I don't do this, I can find myself grieving for something that only ever existed in my mind. I still get sad at the loss of what Sam can't do but I am always reminding myself he was only ever going to do those things in my imagination.

As each birthday approaches, I find myself reflecting on the year gone by. A new year is beginning, what will it hold? Those early years dragged, very, very slowly. With so many traumatic incidents and appointments to mark the weeks, they felt like a lifetime. Each month had a new admission, ambulance ride or dramatic fit and I could see the whole of the past year stretch out behind us.

Friends would express their surprise at how quickly the years had flown by and how they simply couldn't remember life before their baby arrived. That wasn't our reality. Our life was so very different. Our outlook and expectations had so dramatically changed; our lives and future were unrecognisable. As the candles on the cakes grew so did the differences between Sam and his peers. Aged two, his friends were saying words, walking and reaching out for cuddles. By three, they had a character and personality bursting out of them, desperate to be expressed. By four, they were independent little men verbalising their quirky thoughts and unique perspective. Then the first day of school photos hit Facebook and the difference was breath taking.

As time passed, Tim grew bored of going over what happened when Sam was born every time we approached his birthday. It wasn't until I read the novel *The Shack*, that I was able to leave some of those memories behind.

The Shack is one of those awful, brilliant books. It is awful because it is tragic and harrowing. It is also brilliant in the way it explores brokenness, loss, guilt and forgiveness. After reading it I decided I needed to revisit the time of Sam's birth, to immerse myself in it and be ready to see it with open eyes.

I slunk back to the darkness of his room the night before his birth. I looked around, examined my heart and I gazed at the shadows created by the street light on the wall. I dared to peer into my memories and revisit what I had said to Tim. Why hadn't I pursued my own fear? I considered the decisions we had made, then I asked for forgiveness.

With hindsight, it was clear I made a mistake. I should have insisted on going to the hospital. Sam could have been delivered twelve hours earlier if I hadn't worried I was making a fuss. I will never know the impact that decision, the delays at the hospital, or the poor resuscitation had on the outcome, but I chose forgiveness. I had to let go of my own guilt and the blame of others. In doing so, I could stop the rot. I could cut off the bitterness welling in my heart and eating away at me.

I looked back and shone a light of truth into my past. Only then could I focus on the present. I suddenly realised that up until that point everything I did was a desperate scrabble to try and repay Sam for not making the right decision before he was born. Once I acknowledged a level of responsibility, no matter how big or small, only then could I let myself be forgiven.

As a result of this process, and the ensuing years of fits and traumas, I now make decisions knowing I do so based on the information I have; leaving no room for regret.

Whether choosing to leave Sam for the evening or to have a few days away, I deliberately go through all the information in my head. I ensure that every decision I make is based on my best knowledge at the time.

I no longer live believing the consequence proves whether a decision was correct. I may make a right choice and the outcome is disastrous. It is more time consuming, but I make decisions I am least likely to regret. Regret is a cancer as strong as guilt that will eat away and change me beyond all recognition.

A few weeks after Sam's first birthday, I celebrated my thirtieth. I was getting older and fatter; part pregnancy, part cake. Rachel and I had a joint fancy dress party with 'The

London Underground' theme to celebrate. Liz baked a fantastic birthday cake, in true super-mum, WI style, and our friends came dressed in a variety of outfits; from Arsenal shirts to sumo wrestlers (Wapping!).

Tim took a spade and wore wellies while I hired a nun's outfit. It suited me down to the ground and covered my growing bump brilliantly. Together we went as Covent Garden tube station. It was a really fun night with friends and family.

18

Not Feeding: 8th December 2006

"Food is our common ground, a universal experience."
James Beard

I sat holding Sam, aged fourteen months, in a corridor of Great Ormond Street Hospital waiting for the results of a barium swallow test he had just received. Tim couldn't take the time off work, so I was with my mum and littlest sister, Sarah, who had come across London to meet us. I knew from earlier assessments at the hospital, that Sam was not likely to be able to maintain his own nutrition without artificial support. As a result, we were on the waiting list for a permanent tube, called a PEG tube, to be inserted into his stomach, to continue topping up his nutrition after eating.

Before long the speech and language therapist joined us in the corridor. I assumed it was relatively good news, falsely reassured by the fact that we were sitting in a public place with people milling around. The omission of a comfy seat and box of tissues meant I didn't anticipate the need to brace myself.

As passing x-ray trolleys narrowly missed our toes and people sat in chairs alongside, the speech and language therapist began speaking in quiet, thoughtful tones.

"The results of the test are conclusive, but I'm afraid they aren't good."

122

"Ok." I nodded, inviting more information.

"The barium shows Sam's swallow is unsafe. Every time he eats, a small amount of food bypasses his oesophagus and goes into his lungs." A pause.

"To make things worse he doesn't react normally to this by coughing. We call it silent aspiration."

"I see. How do I help him feed?"

"Well our recommendation is that Sam is nil by mouth from now on."

Silence.

I look around the corridor aimlessly before returning to the eyes of the woman speaking.

"What, completely nil by mouth? Not eat anything, ever?" I finally respond.

"Yes, that's our recommendation. Sam has an incredibly high chance of getting a serious chest infection every time he eats."

"Right, I see." My words sounded hollow in the busy corridor.

"Some parents choose to take that risk, feeling their child's quality of life is more important because they love eating."

I glanced up to see my mum's characteristic quivering bottom lip, as she fought back tears. Focusing on the speckled hospital floor, I tried to consider the implications of never feeding Sam again. Inch by inch my maternal roles were being stripped away.

"Well, I guess Sam hasn't ever really enjoyed eating." I fumbled. "He doesn't fight it, but it isn't something he looks forward to."

"Well, it's really your decision, but our recommendation is that he shouldn't have anything by mouth because it is unsafe to do so. We will send you a full report in the post and let your paediatrician know we think Sam needs a PEG as soon as possible. Do you have any questions?"

My mind whirred with questions that couldn't be answered, so instead we talked about the practicalities of not feeding. We discussed the benefits of using a dummy and giving Sam something to bite so that he could experience chewing. At the end of our very brief conversation on a busy corridor in the depths of Great Ormond Street Hospital, we finished with a polite goodbye and got ready to leave. Under my calm exterior, I was feeling how my mum looked: shell-shocked.

I left the hospital once again held up by my mum as we stepped into the cold winter day. While she stayed with Sam, I headed toward Queen Square. I paced amongst the trees with the wind rustling the leaves and biting my ears. My fingers found the fast dial key to Tim.

"Hi, how's it going?" Tim answered brightly.

"We've just left the hospital. It isn't good." I hesitated. "They say we shouldn't feed Sam ever again."

"What?"

I imagined Tim sitting behind his desk at work, in the middle of a busy surgery, trying to soak up the news.

"They have said Sam's swallow isn't safe and we should never feed him again," I reiterated.

As we talked Tim asked questions I had failed to think of, practical issues and challenges for the future, and I felt the unravelling begin once again. My emotions churned within me at how my identity as a mother would be affected by not cooking for or feeding my son.

The call ended with our words frozen in the frigid air. There was no sense of resolution, no feeling that the conversation had finished; we simply paused talking, until another time.

Once again Mum and I had taken the train, not believing we needed the solace of a car journey home. I held my son and gazed out of the smeared glass of the train window. As tower blocks became fields I imagined simple pleasures slipping past becoming faint dots on the horizon.

I recalled bright and fragrant memories of birthday cakes and Grandma Hessie coming to visit every Thursday with a Curly Wurly. Memories of the excitement on hearing the ice-cream van pull into our street or the smell of a bakers danced in my mind. I remembered sitting on the mud floor of a hut in Uganda, as a feast of unrecognisable food was served to the Mzungu guests. So many of my best memories smelt and tasted good. I know what I had for breakfast on my wedding day and what we ate at my twenty-first birthday party. The smell and taste of my world is the flavour and vibrancy of my memories.

What was life without food?

Once home I washed up the feeding utensils we had used for breakfast, opened our broken kitchen drawer and removed all of the baby spoons and forks. I did the same for Sam's cups, bowls, jars of food, and baby crisps. Like a quitting smoker getting rid of paraphernalia, I put out of sight the remnants of an old habit that needed to be broken.

They were boxed and put away, minus a few exceptions left out for visiting babies, ones that could safely swallow. For days to come, each time I opened the drawer or cupboard there they were, a silent reminder.

It was another loss.

The high chair remained around the dining room table because Sam needed to be positioned upright when fed using the nasogastric tube. The tray, however, became a place to put toys instead of food.

Over the succeeding months, we began to learn how to

125

live without feeding Sam. Initially it felt like a gaping hole in our family life together. Our gathering at the table no longer made sense; yet the numbness faded, as it always does.

What remained were the unexpected situations that triggered the crashing waves of grief and stopping me in my tracks. It's the 'firsts' that are the hardest: the first time a waitress gave Sam a menu and waited to hear his order, the first time his friends were given an ice cream as a treat at the beach, the first Christmas dinner he didn't eat and the first birthday cake not shared by the birthday boy.

Over time, I realised much of my pain was tied up in the sense of loss I would feel if someone took away the social pleasure of celebrating and enjoying food with family and friends. There is a strong link between my emotions and my desire to eat chocolate and cake. The news of Sam's inability to eat was a great example as I reacted by delving into sweet foods, trying to comfort my breaking heart. A life without the joy of food felt like a deep loss because I thought Sam was going to miss out on so much of the world I loved. In reality Sam appeared unfazed. He smiled, chuckled and occasionally pulled out the tube in his nose, before fighting the inevitable and uncomfortable reinsertion.

He hadn't loved food and didn't seem to miss it. We occasionally gave him tasters but even they didn't appear to be enjoyed very much. Eating was stressful for him as he struggled to swallow and prevent choking. When Sam drank milk, it poured out the side of his mouth. I accepted this as normal until I realised it was because Sam couldn't coordinate his swallow fast enough. Milk was seeping from his lips because I was effectively forcing milk down his throat too quickly and this was his only way to stop himself choking. No wonder Sam was pleased when he was no longer expected to satisfy his hunger or thirst in this way. While my heart was breaking for what he would miss, Sam appeared relieved.

A couple of weeks later and we celebrated Sam's second Christmas. Belatedly we emailed a Christmas greeting with a photo of the three of us sitting in front of our Christmas tree on the front. It was a classic Christmas greeting photo minus the Christmas jumpers. We were less shell-shocked one year on from Sam's MRI results but our fit-related stress levels were at an all-time high.

By the end of January 2007, after a couple of admissions to St. Thomas's Hospital, Sam finally had a PEG tube inserted into his stomach and we got his 'face back'. There were no more questions about sick babies and no more PH strips. Rather a much easier system of feeding began and another routine with new habits formed.

A new way of life, where tubes and artificial milk were the norm ensued. As a result our little boy didn't suffer repeated chest infections. However, no matter how long we live in this realm, the unanticipated waves of sadness still occasionally come.

Sometimes, all it takes is a chocolate button.

19

I Get Knocked Down: February 2007

*"It's not whether you get knocked down,
it's whether you get up."*

Vince Lombardi

At seven months pregnant I opened the chemist door to hear the loud irritating beep indicating a customer was entering. Walking in backwards, I pushed the door with my back and brought Sam along after me.

"Good morning." I smiled at the kind Sikh pharmacist.

"Morning. Hi Sam, how are you this morning?"

We talked about the medications I came to collect and the changes being proposed by our local consultant. Just as I turned to leave, I was shocked by an unusual question.

"And how are *you* doing?" enquired the pharmacist, looking me straight in the eyes.

My initial surprise turned to awkwardness and confusion, as I was not sure how to answer without referring to Sam. Eventually I talked about struggling with juggling everything, feeling tired and overwhelmed, unsure of what lay around the corner. A short conversation followed before I left with Sam's medications hanging from the pushchair in a plastic bag.

I walked home and reflected on the dozens of people I

interacted with every week. Of all the appointments I attended and numerous professionals I met, I couldn't recall being so directly asked that question before.

When a friend asked me how I was, my response inevitably involved information about Sam. My emotions and strength were dictated by how Sam was doing or the crisis we had just survived.

I felt defined and identified by Sam's disability. It was evolving with time and permeating even more of our lives. Nothing was resilient to its impact. Whether it was how Sam ate, sat, looked or slept, something always needed doing or changing. His body couldn't be trusted. Without intervention his muscles would tighten, limbs retract and body deform. As more changes were made, more problems arose and needed to be prevented.

When living moment to moment I enjoyed life and my son but when I stopped and looked around, I found myself flanked by frustration and exhaustion. I was constantly knocked back by new difficulties. I wished someone would tell me exactly what life would be like, what precisely we were dealing with and how Sam would develop. At least then I could try and deal with it, once and for all. As weeks turned into months, then years, I realised, that as much as the battering was exhausting, if it had come all at once I simply wouldn't have got up again.

At times life felt like it was being lived in a boxing ring. I learnt some fancy new footwork but still life's blows descended, solid and strong. Instantly I would buckle, hitting the canvas with surprising ease. Sometimes the recovery was slow; while at other times my son's smile or dirty snigger dragged me to my feet, even before the referee had counted to four.

The most challenging blows, though, were the sucker punches; the knocks inflicted when I was distracted or completely unprepared. Anticipating a difficult situation enabled me to prepare myself. Then suddenly something would strike out of the blue, taking the wind out of me as I dropped to the canvas unable to recover. Watching a toddler in his wellington boots splashing in muddy puddles had once rendered me crushed and ready to throw in the towel.

My greatest challenge, though, was my lack of contender. I had no one, or nothing, to throw a punch at. No opponent to focus my anger on. I didn't have a cancer to fight or abusive relationship to escape. The source of my most challenging and painful emotions was also the focus of my greatest affection. Tied up in Sam were my deepest love, purest joy, greatest heartache and darkest suffering. Within our relationship, these conflicting emotions were required to sit together in harmony. Each one intricately entwined to create the unique bond between us: mother and son.

Our local postman has been known to land a blow.

In my little boxing ring, where I'm shifting my feet and dancing around trying to avoid being hit, the postman often comes to the ropes and lands a punch with a letter. Sam gets more post than anyone else in our house. Sometimes I don't even have to open it for the pain to be felt, as the envelope is emblazoned with words like 'Together for shorter lives'. The truth that Sam isn't expected to live to adulthood is a reality, but getting a letter from a fantastic charity supporting families like ours, brings the hard truth to my doorstep whether I'm prepared for it or not.

One such sucker punch landed when I took Sam for a routine eye appointment. I went to the hospital on my own. The initial part involved a friendly young woman and several seemingly random checks. She waved a pencil, with a furry

130

bobble at the end, in front of Sam's eyes and did the same with small flashing lights. I didn't need any training to know that things weren't great, but that was no surprise. We then waited in the corridor and I chatted to Sam about what was going on. I was beginning to get quite good at having both sides of a conversation all by myself.

"Samuel Wright?" called a slightly small, friendly looking ophthalmologist.

"Hi, take a seat. Can you hold him on your knee please." More tests were carried out and after a few short minutes he turned around, smiled and handed me a sheet of A4 paper.

"So, as we've discussed before, Sam's *eyes* work fine but the part of his brain that interprets his sight is badly damaged."

A nod was all that was required.

"So I've filled out this form which registers him blind."

"O... kay." My sharp intake of breath indicated my shock.

"That isn't anything you haven't been told already is it?"

The nerves from my ears took the 'blind' message through my brain, while a droplet of sadness seeped into my heart and took residence. It began unpacking its things and prepared to stay for the foreseeable future. Meanwhile, words of platitude that betrayed my emotions flowed out of my mouth with seamless ease.

"No, no, of course not. Thank you."

"I don't think there is any real point in seeing Sam again, so I will discharge him from my clinic."

"Yes, of course," I chirped, with a smile.

"If you have any future concerns, see your GP or consultant and you can be referred back, I'd be more than happy to see you again."

"That's great. Er... Thank very much."

Clearly our appointment time was finished. A few more

smiles were shared as I lifted Sam from my knee and placed him in his pushchair.

As I stepped out of the ophthalmology department, the sliding doors closed behind us and the cold air hit. It had been cold for a long time. The day was grey and damp. I gazed down at Sam who had turned his head to one side in disapproval of the change in atmosphere. I attached his pushchair's rain cover to protect him from the worsening weather and began to walk.

The doctor was right. I hadn't been told anything I didn't already know. However, the folded sheet of paper that declared Sam blind now sat heavily in his baby bag and my own growing backpack of emotions. I realised that already knowing the truth doesn't stop it landing like a haymaker. A punch destined as a knock out.

Sam was blind.

He couldn't see me when I walked in the room. He wasn't able to gaze into my eyes and connect with me. He missed the ability to make sense of all the colours and beauty around him. This truth had always been there, sitting discreetly and unassuming at the bottom of my rucksack, but that day and the following days it grew in magnitude and mass. The heaviness dug into my back leaving me fatigued.

I scrambled in my pocket for my mobile phone and tried to call Tim with no luck, so I called my mum in Buckingham. As I started to speak, I began to weep. I wept for what Sam was missing, what we couldn't share and how helpless I was. On the other end of the phone Mum mourned with me as we walked home with the biting wind drying my tears. Mum and Dad's plans to move to Southend were coming together but right at that moment the next six months couldn't pass fast enough.

Grief is easier shared.

Then in 2007 hope arrived.

She came in the form of our first visit to the Bobath Centre. For two weeks we abused the hospitality of our good friends, Will and Jess, living in Muswell Hill whilst daily making the five-minute journey to East Finchley for an hour and a half of therapy.

By the end of two weeks at Bobath, Sam moved his hand to indicate he wanted to hear more music. Suddenly using a switch as a form of communication became possible. This was revolutionary. We began to see that Sam had preferences. We were taught not to dumb down our language, but reflect back all that Sam did and how we interpreted his actions. Rather than being given a list of activities to perform, we were taught principles that affected how we interacted with Sam. Instead of focusing on vision or physiotherapy, we saw our whole son and the potential of what he could do in various situations.

Another window had been thrown open.

Once home, small interactions became commonplace. After his bath Sam lay on his changing mat, looked across at his music and vocalised. Sam was communicating. Our little boy, with his soft round cheeks and blazing blue eyes, was talking.

"What are you trying to say Sam? Do you want your music on?" I would ask.

A smile would creep across Sam's face as noise passed his lips and his knees would rise in excitement.

"You're telling me, yes. You're smiling and saying yes. Ok, let me put on your music," I would say through my own smile.

Before long we got into a routine of Sam 'asking' for his music and lights. Before bed, I would read him his bedtime story and at the end of a page I would wait for Sam to raise his hand indicating he wanted me to turn the page. The relief at communicating with Sam was immense. It was limited but it was there.

So often, it had felt as though Sam lived encased in cotton wool, buffeted from life. Yet these moments of interaction pierced through those outer layers and briefly I connected with my son. We heard each other and responded to one another. Our relationship had been founded on love, now there was a glimpse of understanding too.

The fight was worth it and the victory incredible.

My boy wanted to talk to me.

20

Take 2: 11th April 2007

"I hope everything turns out ok, otherwise I don't think I could cope."
A friend

As I neared the end of pregnancy, my emotions were frayed. My wonderful grandma had a great habit of saying 'God willing'. Whether she was making plans to visit her son in New Zealand or arranging to be collected for church next Sunday, she'd often finish with 'God willing'. Daily she proclaimed God was in control.

Tim's grandad was an archetypal fine old gentleman. I only ever remember him wearing a shirt, usually a tie, and always ready with a tale relevant to any situation. When thinking about the future he would quip, 'Expect the worst and hope for the best'. Although my faith is more in line with Grandma's, when it came to my second pregnancy, my attitude reflected Grandad's.

Three months earlier I had met Tim just inside the sliding doors of the women's clinic for our twenty-week scan. We stepped out of the cold air into the familiar muggy atmosphere of the hospital and followed the signs.

Sitting in the waiting area we chatted. Posters on the wall warned against the dangers of smoking and the need to remove any belly buttons rings. The free water from a cooling system in the corner ensured bladders were full and ready. This level of thoughtfulness continued right up to providing a sweet machine, packed with the crisps and chocolate essential for every pregnant woman.

Looking around I analysed the other women and partners sitting expectantly on the same coarse, red chairs. I looked at their families with envy. Healthy toddlers ran around, while mothers seemingly blossomed, gently resting hands on their growing bumps.

I wonder if I look like that, I thought, *or does my body language divulge my fears?*

So many people had asked us if we were going to find out the sex of our baby. I got bored of reminding them that the primary role of a twenty-week scan was to check the health of a fetus.

"Rachel Wright?" called a slim lady with mousy brown, curly hair.

Her stark white uniform was as angular and precise as her pointy nose. She was kind and friendly, trying to make us feel at ease. We were relieved to be told so far so good, but then we had been here before. After paying £2 for a fuzzy black and white print of our baby, we went across to wait to see the consultant.

He welcomed us in with a grin. Knowing what happened with Sam we discussed the options available to minimise it happening again. A couple of extra scans were booked and I was given open access to the antenatal ward. I worried about how stressful the last two weeks of pregnancy would be, knowing that Sam's brain damage occurred during this time. The consultant agreed he would personally undertake an elective caesarean section on 12th April 2007, two weeks before the baby was due and exactly eighteen months after Sam was born. If I went into labour beforehand, we could decide whether to try a normal delivery or have an emergency caesarean.

As time drew on, friends and family tried to reassure us that all was well but I was finding it increasingly hard. I was keen to remind them my pregnancy with Sam had been textbook right up until the last day.

Then several weeks before our baby was due we found ourselves in Milton Keynes General. Once again, we were curled up together in a hospital bed and darkened room.

For the past few days we had been staying at my mum and dad's, in Buckingham. Tim had a week's study leave from his job as a GP registrar and was studying for his GP exams in a caravan in their garden. He needed time and space to work without interruption, but he didn't feel Sam's condition could be trusted enough for him to actually go away anywhere.

I began to notice minor abdominal tightening. It wasn't unusual given the stage of my pregnancy but what became worrying was their frequency and regularity. Although not particularly painful, my stomach hardened and I felt uncomfortable every five minutes. So we called the delivery suite at Milton Keynes and ended up being admitted for observation.

It was late in the evening when we got there and the place was heaving. We were shown to a room where I was quickly strapped to a monitor. All appeared fine but they could see my small contractions occurring. Within a couple of hours a doctor came to see us.

"We are concerned you may be going into early labour."

We didn't speak, just nodded.

"The safest course of action is for you to have a steroid injection just in case the baby is born early."

"OK." More nodding and gripping onto Tim's hand.

"Unfortunately we don't have any intensive care beds available for a premature baby so we are looking into transferring you to another hospital."

Was this really happening?

"I'm afraid it's a very busy night so it may not happen quickly but I'll prescribe the steroid now. Any problems just press the buzzer."

The doctor left and we dissected what was happening. When no one returned and the pain didn't get any worse we dozed on and off for the rest of the night. The noises in the corridor indicated it really was hectic on the ward and no one returned.

The next morning the contractions had eased and we were grateful the busy labour ward had resulted in us not being seen again. We were discharged without a steroid injection and our baby securely in place.

This episode jolted me into realising I needed to do some baby preparation. Reluctantly we sourced a double buggy, although I made sure we could take it back without a quibble. A good friend had tried to return a car seat to a shop after one of her twins died at birth but the shop keeper tried to make her buy something else instead. The insensitivity is harrowing.

I dug out Sam's plain sleep suits and borrowed a crib. I wouldn't move Sam into his new room and create a nursery until after the baby was born. As the birth drew closer, the anxieties grew. I ended up back on the antenatal ward a couple of times just wanting reassurance and was always greeted with considerate and sensitive staff.

Unsurprisingly, I monitored my baby's movements religiously. When I woke through the night, I would immediately hold my breath. First, I listened out to hear Sam not fitting on the baby monitor and then I waited patiently to feel my baby move. Each time I returned to sleep, satisfied my baby was active but in the darkness, my wondering thoughts magnified and distorted.

On the morning of Wednesday 11th April I woke, got Sam dressed and kissed Tim goodbye. Before lunch, I found myself reluctantly packing a bag for the baby. I was concerned my waters may have broken and needed to go to the antenatal ward. My dad and mum came from the local campsite they were staying in (it was three months before they moved to Southend). Mum stayed with Sam, while Dad took me to the hospital. My large bump and I clambered into the car as my heart throbbed and bounded in my chest, while my stomach twisted and turned. I so wanted this experience to be different from the first.

So far, it was different. This time I was nervous - last time I was relatively oblivious. This time I could feel my baby move, last time my belly lay silent. This time Tim was working as a GP registrar in a local surgery, no longer working in the hospital. This time I was struggling with old memories.

"Hi, I called earlier. My name is Rachel Wright," I explained to the midwife behind the desk on the antenatal ward.

"Rachel, come with me."

Once settled on a bed a monitor confirmed all appeared fine and an examination showed my waters hadn't broken. I didn't need to wait long to see our consultant. He reassured me again and offered to deliver me later that day. A consultant anaesthetist in the hospital kindly agreed to come up to assist with the caesarean section, once his list in theatre had finished. I called Tim and told him he needed to leave work early. He was going to have a baby, today.

From then on events unfolded in a familiar way. I was transferred to the labour ward, Tim got into his blues and we were taken into the same theatre.

My admiration for my husband multiplied. He had managed to return to this place every day for six months. The same smells, lights and noises of eighteen months earlier filled my senses. I hadn't been back since Sam was born and I was finding it difficult to shake the memories and settle my nerves. A doctor got out the biggest needle I had seen since I was last there and decided the best place for it was my spine. That still seemed like a really stupid idea. If I'd thought it would've helped, I would have supplied flashing lights and a neon sign.

Soon my legs were numb and flopped into position. Tim and I chatted as lightheartedly as we could and distracted ourselves by discussing whether it was appropriate to take a photo over the blue screen when the baby was born. Tim wasn't intending on looking over, he just planned on pointing his phone's camera over the top to capture the moment of extraction. I wasn't sure I wanted to see the inside of my own stomach but I was keen to see it happen.

As before, all was calm and quiet. Lights glared and professionals busied themselves around us. The air filled with the sound of metal on metal. The clattering and chinking was orchestrating a melody of impending change. Amidst it all, I quietly spoke to Tim. No screaming, shouting, sweating or pushing occurred.

A few minutes after 5pm our baby boy was born, weighing half an ounce more than seven pounds. Tim caught the moment on his mobile phone, as a skinny blue baby was removed. His arms and legs splayed out stiff and pointing in all directions. Tim declined cutting the cord and headed to the resuscitaire. Then the similarities stopped.

Our son cried.

He cried loud and clear.

My heart melted at the most amazing sound I had ever heard. I wept unreservedly, with complete and utter joy and relief. Glancing over to the medical staff around my baby, I caught the eye of Sam's consultant who was grinning from ear to ear with his thumbs up. Before long, Tim brought my wrapped little baby boy and I kissed his head and face, again and again and again.

He lay on my chest slimy and noisy. Our baby was delicate and precise. He had a fine covering of fair hair and wrinkled skin on his fingers that boasted long white fingernails. I was once again overwhelmed with new and extraordinary emotions.

Tim kissed me and we looked at each other as tears continued to fall. This was a different path, a different experience and a whole new world. It took a while for the doctors to sew me back up and I lost nearly a litre and a half of blood. The obstetrician kindly sorted out my slightly wonky scar, although to my disappointment he didn't go so far as doing a nip and tuck while he was there.

We got word out to our family and friends that we had another son and that 'mother and baby were well'. Those words had become, and will always be, precious. Soon I was sitting up in recovery holding my baby and the differences just kept on coming.

This little boy wriggled, fidgeted, squirmed and cried. I put him to my breast and for the first time realised Sam had never suckled properly. This baby felt more like the breast pump on full speed than what I had experienced with Sam. He fed with ease and I sat smiling, gazing at my boy and his scrunched up nose. I then noticed how tense I had become. Unwittingly, I had been holding every muscle tight and expectant as though standing on a cliff edge. Suddenly, I could step back from the drop off, take a deep breath and feel the ground beneath my feet.

Once I had recovered from the anaesthetic my bed was pushed past the Butterfly Suite and into a side room on the postnatal ward. My parents visited with Sam wearing an 'I'm a big brother t-shirt' and we smiled, cried and hugged. I felt overwhelming love and protection towards Sam and glimpsed the potential of loving another person with the same unconditional passion. Before the end of the evening our minister and his wife, and then Rachel visited. They were all keen to hold our boy and share in our joy.

By the end of the evening, Tim and I were left with our baby discussing names and taking dozens of photos. The only real contender was Jonah. We decided our lives and our family needed a heavy dose of peace.

21

Jonah

Jonah \j(o)-nah\ as a boy's name is pronounced JOE-nah.
It is of Hebrew origin, and the meaning of Jonah is "Dove".
Also means "Peace" as the dove is a symbol of peace.

Like every other father, Tim left the postnatal ward at eight o'clock and I spent the night in my own little room, with a buzzer by my side. I was relieved not to be on the main ward sharing stories and experiences, and although Tim had gone, I didn't feel alone.

I sat on my starched hospital bed holding my tiny soft baby. We talked and hugged as I dreamed of all that might be. I didn't deliberately imagine him sitting or walking or his first day at school, but the expanding future and potentials ahead of him filled the room and my heart. It was breathtakingly different from Sam's stifling and uncertain birth.

I knew I couldn't predict the lives of either of my boys but their trajectories were completely different. I looked into the eyes of my son and said his name over and over.

"Hello Jonah, I'm your mummy. I'm sorry you've had a rough day today. It is very wonderful to meet you. I have been very excited about you coming. Hopefully we'll get you out of this stinky hospital and take you home really soon."

Through the night, I grimaced with discomfort and gingerly cared for my baby. Tentatively I held, fed and talked to him with a weary smile on my face. The next morning I texted Tim details of all the things I wanted at the hospital. The midwife came in and mistakenly believed Jonah had slept through, because I hadn't used the buzzer. I was keen to leave and did everything I could to show we should be discharged as soon as possible. Although I felt tired and woozy I kept it to myself, instead walking around the ward as much as possible, proving I was ready to go home.

On Friday morning a junior doctor examined Jonah and found everything to be normal. I was given iron tablets to help replace some of the blood I lost and we were both discharged with a clean bill of health.

Tim drove us home. He took a photo of me holding Jonah in the same car seat Sam had used on his discharge but it all felt very new. Before I had believed that what my peers went through was different and now I *knew* it wasn't the same.

Our little family woke up on Saturday morning ready for the mayhem of hardly any sleep, numerous visitors and scrabbling around for a routine. We juggled nappies and feeds (breast and PEG), winding and sleeps. It appeared to be a four-man job or at a push, two-women. How on earth was I going to do it on my own?

All was going well until we went to sleep on Saturday night. Doubts started to creep in. Jonah's skull had started to develop the same defined suture lines Sam had at just after a few days old. We believed the shrinking of Sam's damaged brain had caused the pronounced dip in his head. Now we were beginning to see the same disturbing feature on top of Jonah's skull. We kept his little hat on and the secret of our fears close to our chest.

144

Family and friends visited and cooed, while we smiled and feared the worst. On Sunday, we discussed our concerns with Mum and Dad. Our minds were spinning and my emotions felt flighty and unhinged. On Sunday evening, Mum looked after the boys while Tim and I went for a walk along the marshes at Two Tree Island.

The evening was relatively warm and I tentatively walked along, leaning on Tim's arm. We couldn't understand how it had happened but we convinced ourselves it had. Our son must have brain damage.

"Maybe we only do boys with brain damage." Tim's words cut through the peaceful air.

"I know I can do it if I have to but I just can't imagine coping with the grief and pain all over again. I guess I have an idea of what's in store though."

Warily my feet tread the thin, muddy walkway.

"What on earth are we going to tell people? How do we break the news?"

We talked and laid our emotions and fears bare. For the millionth time I was grateful to be going through all of this with my best friend and the most wonderful man I know.

We made a plan to call Sam's consultant first thing Monday morning and ask him to examine Jonah. That night we held each other, this time in our own bed, and as I fed Jonah in the darkness, I tried to stop the clawing oppression of my thoughts.

By lunchtime on Monday, we left the paediatric ward having had Jonah examined. The consultant told us, in no uncertain terms, that Jonah was a perfectly normal healthy newborn and we had absolutely nothing to fear. A second wave of relief swept over us, stilling our hearts and minds. We walked out of the ward and never looked back.

Jonah felt different, fed differently, held differently and sounded different. He looked different and we handled him differently. Looking after him was a breeze and I quickly noticed how much easier it was caring for a baby without added emotions of grief and uncertainty. Within a few days, we were meeting with friends at the beach for picnics and enjoying being a family.

Once Tim was back at work, a rota my friend Alex had organised kicked in. I was incredibly grateful for the numerous people who took turns in helping me with Sam while I wasn't allowed to lift him. Then once I was given the all clear, I started taking responsibility for both the boys on my own. Thankfully, it wasn't long before my parents moved to Southend and their continuing help became invaluable.

The pace with which Jonah changed was startling, every little development took us by surprise as we cherished every moment. Skills that still remain difficult to Sam were effortless. The first time I walked into the room and Jonah's eyes sparkled at me with recognition and delight, my own swelled with tears. When he reached out for me to pick him up, it was like a miracle. Then at a few months old, I was astounded when he sat up. His firm straight spine was truly amazing.

I was also surprised that no sooner had the mashing and blending of baby food begun, when Jonah too began to glow. He showed the undeniable tinge of orange seen only eighteen months earlier in his older sibling. I suspect both boys have a mutant 'orange' gene, one that is triggered by a minor excess of carotene. I might enlist them into the Xavier Institute where they can be trained with all the other X-men; the school is already wheelchair adapted.

As the physical milestones were ticked off, Jonah's personality came out loud and strong. He is as laid back and

146

inquisitive as his dad, showing his tendency to be a geek and want absolutely everything explained. Where Sam has Tim's hair, Jonah has his everything else.

*

Jonah brings so much life and love into our lives and never stops making us smile. His relationship with Sam is unique, although watching him deal with the reality of his brother's limitations is painful at times. When out with Jonah on our own, he always notices the ramps and disabled adaptations saying,

"See, we could have brought Sammy."

He was only three years old when he first asked me why God let Sam be born with a broken brain. It was during shower time and I handled the situation particularly well. I paused, looked him straight in the eyes and clamoured, "Oh look, we've run out of shampoo. I'll just go and get some more."

Once I had prepared myself (being a good mum isn't natural; I had to have time to think about it) we discussed his question the next day. By the time he was five Jonah was able to articulate himself a bit better. One evening I was busy cooking dinner, while Sam watched TV, and Jonah looked at me quizzically. I stopped and indicated I was ready to listen to what he had to say.

"I'm trying to work out the mystery of why Sammy was born too early. At the time that made him disabled. And I was born at a time when I'm like me. He was born at the wrong time," he said, in broken but clear sentences.

"He wasn't born at the wrong time," I reassured. "He was born at the right time."

I paused, allowing the truth of those simple words to seep

into my own heart.

"Sam was born on the day the doctors expected," I explained.

"So why didn't it happen to me?"

Slowly I walked across the kitchen to hold Jonah.

"Something happened in the week before Sammy was born that hurt his brain and made it not work so well. So when you were in my belly the doctor decided to take you out early so that didn't happen."

"Why didn't you take Sammy out early?"

Silence and welling eyes dominated my face, while innocence and expectation pervaded Jonah's.

"If I'd known darling, I would have, but I didn't know."

22

Tim's Story

France: 13th August 2007

"Change is as good as a holiday."

A proverb

Stark blue moonlight streaked through the small, deep-set window in the rural French cottage owned by Tim's uncle and aunt, Malcolm and Beate. Tim rested against the coarse whitewashed brickwork as he held Sam in his arms and tried to adjust his senses. As the frigid light broke through the thick warm air, he felt a million miles from home, yet the scenario was all too familiar.

The sense of holiday had turned sour that evening the instant Sam developed a fever. The morphing from relaxed father, to on-call doctor happened as smoothly as Clarke Kent turning into Superman in a phone box. After only two days in France, Tim found himself rocking his hot son; fervently praying over his little body. As he swayed and soothed the journey so far swept across his mind like a movie reel.

We had narrowly avoided missing our flight because it took so long to get a gallon of liquid medications through security. But quickly the family had settled into the rustic

149

French cottage set in idyllic countryside, surrounded by fields of sunflowers. He recalled the family day out, with the stalls and smells of the traditional village fete visited earlier that day. Then the unscripted film-like sequence abruptly ended, bringing Tim to the dark, hot and unpredictable present, rocking his feverish limp son.

It had been months since Sam was admitted to hospital; a short respite since Jonah was born four months earlier. Clinically Tim had done everything possible. As a father his only remaining arsenal was prayer. As though in a trance he prayed silently with passion over Sam, his rosary beads becoming the rhythmical stroking of his son's hot brow. When Tim's thoughts stopped forming words, a consequence of spiritual and emotional fatigue, his heart took over with mumbling groans and impassioned pleas of healing and protection. For hours after everyone else fell asleep he stayed awake and prayed.

Then his voice punctured the darkness, "Rachel, wake up!" he called.

"Rachel, Sam's fitting. We need to call an ambulance."

In a haze of sleep I jumped out of bed and stormed into Malcolm and Beate's bedroom, requesting they call an ambulance. Beate flew downstairs and called the number she had searched out the day before, just in case. Silently we hurried around, Tim giving the rescue medication, while I dressed, packed a bag and collected the relevant medical and insurance documents.

When the ambulance finally arrived I climbed inside with Sam and Beate, whose fluent French was desperately needed. Tim remained in the cottage, scurrying around collecting everything else we might need before packing Jonah into his car seat and heading towards the hospital. Tim gripped the steering wheel and leaned forward, straining to see the blackened country lanes ahead. His heart raced as he focused on following Malcolm's car. The darkness enveloped him as the tightening in his chest grew while adrenaline pushed aside any feelings of fatigue.

Eventually, he found Sam on the paediatric ward, still fitting. Beate and I had failed to persuade the medical staff the small boy flinching and shaking needed urgent medical attention. Some two hours after the fit had begun clonapezam was finally administered orally and the seizure subsided.

While I fed Jonah on the ward, Tim took Sam down for an EEG. He sat once again, cradling his sleeping son, as electrodes were secured to his scalp. The EEG had only just begun when Sam's muscles began jumping and jolting once again.

"Excuse me," Tim shouted towards the EEG technician, who appeared oblivious to the escalating situation. "Can you help, please?" Only a nod of recognition came. "He is fitting. We need to stop the EEG."

Finally the technician came into the room and hurriedly removed the electrodes. Tim sped back to the ward with Sam and the print out of sharp peaks and troughs showing the violent activity in his brain.

Once a neurologist on the ward saw Sam and the EEG, medical staff finally leapt into action and Sam was rushed to a specialist room in the basement of the hospital. Several medical staff descended and began attaching lines and getting out needles when we were asked to leave the room. As a foreign doctor, Tim had no power or influence. It seemed in France, he had even less significance as a parent.

In an eerily deserted corridor, in the belly of a French hospital time hobbled forward fitful and disjointed, as we waited to hear if our son had died. Tim stood under the bright strobe lighting holding me, comfortable in his role as husband.

After fifteen minutes a tall, slim doctor wearing dark rimmed glasses and a white coat, strode into the corridor.

"He is still fitting."

"Yes, he has bad fits and needs a needle in the vein to give lorazepam to stop them." Tim instructed, for the hundredth time.

"We are trying to get vein but no good. We try intraosseous next."

Tim shot me a look, hoping I didn't know what that meant, yet my fear stained eyes betrayed my understanding, as they swelled with tears.

"Ok, I understand. He needs lorazepam."

The doctor nodded, turned and swept back into the room where Sam lay.

"Come here." Tim gently drew me in, as I quietly began weeping. We stood together imagining the large metal needle being inserted into our son's bone; a technique used as a last resort to get essential medicine into a dying child.

After a while, muffled screams were heard snaking down the corridor. Tim's role was now reduced to security guard, as he prevented me from barging into the room to see what was happening. Time seemed to stand still before we heard the heels of the same doctor progressing back along the corridor.

"You can come now. Good news. Medicine in the vein through the neck. But fit too long. Need go to a new hospital."

We stepped into the room busied with medics. Sam lay lifeless on a bed, with a needle secured into his neck and a ventilator strapped to his mouth. Machines around us whirred and bleeped, as news of a helicopter transfer to intensive care at the regional hospital was communicatd in broken English. There would not be room for us in the helicopter; Sam would have to go alone. With little pomp and ceremony we were instructed to kiss Sam goodbye, unsure if we would hold him again.

In the early morning light we waited in the hospital car park as Malcolm brought our suitcases from the cottage. Once we had loaded the car with our belongings, I jumped in the driver's seat and Tim gathered a map and scribbled directions. Instinctively gazing up to scan the sky for hospital helicopters, Tim tried to distract himself with the task of finding the location of our son. Planning the route, trying to appear calm and in control, he felt fear rising in his throat like foul bile, scorching and painful. Gripped with anxiety he gave sharp clear directions as little talking interrupted the two-hour drive.

Down a small side street I parked the hire car and we hurried to find Sam. At the entrance to intensive care we were told to wait. Four hours after we kissed our son goodbye we stepped into the intensive care side room, having left Jonah enjoying the company of the ward receptionist. For the rest of the day we took turns visiting Sam who remained stable but on a ventilator. That night Jonah slept in his pushchair while Tim and I shared another hospital bed. A day later, Sam had improved enough to be moved to a regular ward where Tim once again lay holding his son.

Examining Sam's peaceful expression, Tim was deeply grateful that he at least, would have little memory of the last two days. Although the mild fevers continued, all investigations had proved negative to anything serious. Slowly sliding his arm from under Sam's head, Tim slipped off the bed and stepped toward the large window. Holding a polystyrene cup containing lukewarm tea, he surveyed the city skyline. The lights illuminated the night and blotted out the stars he had dreamed of gazing.

Turning his back to his unforeseen holiday destination, Tim looked towards the hot, oppressive hospital room. So much looked familiar; the same hospital bed, starched sheets and cardiac monitor hooked up to the same fragile life. His eyes rested on a little boy who consumed his emotions and dragged him into a new world of boundless love and stress.

A nurse stepped into Sam's room to take his temperature, dissipating the sense of familiarity. Using rusty GCSE French Tim smiled a greeting but failed to have enough vocabulary to engage in any friendly banter, or find out the most recent blood results. His stammering communication stoked feelings of isolation and powerlessness. This was normally his world, his territory, yet he felt like an alien. Up until now, travelling had been about submerging into new cultures. However, he would have happily skipped experiencing this aspect of authentic French living.

A week later, in a bustling, cramped airport terminal, Tim hugged Sam in his arms on French soil for the last time. He nervously entertained him whilst waiting to board the plane home. Silently hoping Sam's temperature didn't rise, he sang *The Grand Old Duke of York* for the umpteenth time while gently bouncing him on his knee. After a short delay, the whole family piled onto the plane.

During take-off Tim scanned the landscape below while continuing his endless renditions of nursery rhymes. As the fields and houses took on the form of a Legoland world, he allowed his shoulders to lower, relieved he was finally making way towards a world he understood and in which he wielded more control.

The day before, Tim had sat outside the cottage's red stable door with a beer in his hand, his heart breaking at what could have been a week of relaxation and renewal. Yet the local country lanes were left unexplored.

As the plane tracked its journey back to the UK, the horizon began to shrink. With each mile closer to home, Tim couldn't imagine ever having the courage, or holiday insurance, to take his family out of the country again. Adjusting to not living in a developing country had been a challenge but now he faced never taking his family out of England.

The weariness of living without a break sank in. Weekends weren't restful because caring for Sam entailed a constant stream of tasks. Holidays too had become a change of scenery, rather than a rest. The specialist equipment used to make life easier was left at home and now so many destinations and views had slipped out of reach.

As the plane touched down, Tim looked up and caught my eye. In one wordless glance, the sense of relief and disappointment between us was palpable. Later, as he stepped out of arrivals, Tim failed to dampen his feelings of being tied to Essex in order to keep his family safe. It was the end of another era; no longer could we simply tweak life a little to make it suit us.

Yet as he passed open fields and the familiar landscapes, Tim's most overwhelming emotion was gratitude. He was grateful that he was coming home with his family intact.

Part 3
Learning to Live
Again

23

Acceptance

*"The same boiling water softens potatoes and hardens eggs.
It's all about what you're made of, not your circumstances."*

Unknown

In the years after Jonah was born, there were so many happy moments, trials and lessons. We had some routine and lots of fun. Tim came home from work in time for a quick rough and tumble before bed (with the boys not me). Occasionally I would boost the efforts of the younger members of the family to balance the scales. I was glad there were others in the house for Tim to inflict his tickling on.

In the summer of 2007 my parents moved to Southend and became important members of our pit crew, while I managed to perfect a very good Roadrunner impression. As though being chased down by the crafty Wile E Coyote, my bright blue head darted about everywhere, with my whirring legs sweeping up a cloud of sand.

I wanted to be a great mum to Sam. I wanted to care for him well and give him the necessary therapies. I wanted to be a fun mum for Jonah. I wanted to continue to work as a nurse and be a good wife to Tim. I wanted to love well and live in line with my faith and values. Trying to maintain all of the expectations I had of myself was impossible.

My days were consumed with tasks. When Jonah was younger, I had the hope of him becoming more independent. I pushed myself through each stage of development believing the next era would be easier. I hoped for a better tomorrow and pushed myself beyond sustainability into exhaustion. I started the long trend of building a deficit of energy, finishing each day more spent than filled.

To all but those very close to me, I appeared to do a pretty good job. I was coping and smiling as I shakily headed off down the rugged path of acceptance. It's a cliché but true, that acceptance is a journey not a destination. Acceptance Avenue is full of steep ascents and few descents with various milestones and monuments decorating its route. Yet with Jonah's growing character and Sam's smile, I saw the bright side of life although the painful differences were never far away. It wasn't long before Jonah overtook Sam developmentally, as though Spock had hit hyper drive. Every day he seemed to show us something new he had learnt and within twelve months he was light years ahead.

Jonah took his first steps quite late as he decided talking was a more vital skill, chattering and muttering all day long. Over time, incoherent mumblings became exuberant explanations, then excuses, and to date, he still doesn't stop talking. One evening, when he was about three, I asked Jonah to tidy his toys off the floor. He politely explained that he couldn't because God had told him not to. In fact, God had sent his son Jesus and told him not to tidy his toys. I would have told him off if it hadn't been for the fact that I was rolling around with laughter.

The reality of Jonah developing beyond my own thoughts was a revelation. No matter how old Sam becomes he remains dependent upon others for everything, including his communication. Sam too is sociable and bubbly, 'mmming' and 'aaahing', hopeful for a conversation. Over time, he has developed a limited form of communicating that relies on others interpreting his noises and making assumptions about his desires and requests.

There is a fine balance between accepting Sam and all his limitations, while keeping an open mind about what he may achieve. Discovering that Sam can do something new, or has gained understanding, often occurs by accident. We realised he could control going to the toilet when, aged four, he took to deliberately farting on my mum's knee to make her laugh. This showed both Sam's physical control and his sense of humour. I decided if he could squeeze out a fart for comic effect, he could go to the toilet on demand. Together, we embarked on a very long journey of toilet training.

As Sam grew, there were many obstacles along my road of acceptance. Initially I took both boys out in a double buggy, with the local wheelchair service providing crafted bits of foam and cloth. Then specialist equipment was required and even they needed bespoke adaptations. Today I use various people in my local area to help me adapt and customise equipment and clothing for Sam: it remains a team effort.

With time the impact of Sam's disability spread, permeating every aspect of life like yeast. I remember visiting Judie in the toy library after hearing we needed to lay Sam in a sleep system at night. He already had specialist equipment for every eventuality through the day and now the night needed modifications too.

I slumped into a plastic chair as Judie handed me a cup of tea and I cried at nothing being the same. Nothing in Sam's life escaped the grasp of disability, or resembled Jonah's. For him, everything was harder and more complicated.

The reality of all the disabled equipment Sam was beginning to need was like a foghorn screaming 'disabled boy, different from everyone else'. The fact that it all tended to be so ugly and cumbersome didn't help.

Technology has advanced at such a rapid rate that my iPhone can do more in the palm of my hand, than our Commodore Amiga 500k growing up. Yet every disability-related tool or device that crossed our threshold was bulky and resembled a piece of medieval torture equipment. When Sam's high chair no longer suited his needs, it was replaced with a large wooden chair with straps and footplates. When the double buggy wasn't supporting him enough we had to resort to a fully specialised wheelchair, with protruding headrest and a four-point harness, supportive enough to rocket him into space.

The process of trying to get the right equipment was long and often required phone calls, letters and arguing. Yet I didn't really want the equipment in my home. I didn't want the reminder of what Sam couldn't do and how different he was from his brother.

Local therapists gave me links to equipment websites that caused me to wince at its unsightly, disabled appearance. But, as Thomas Hardy said, 'time changes everything except the thing inside us that is surprised by change'. For me it took years, but like the thawing frozen landscape of my mind, I started seeing beauty where I once saw brokenness. Today a wheelchair isn't a contraption that contains or segregates; it's a vehicle of opportunity and integration. My son's neckerchiefs are simply part of his wardrobe. I have gone from recoiling at specialist equipment to seeing it as a positive extension of my son's body; part of him, who he is and who we are as a family.

And to those of you who are at the beginning of this road, please don't fret, rather be kind to yourself. It feels like such a long way off, but just like aching joints, wrinkled skin and greying hair, life and your perspective changes without you even noticing. Time will take you hand-in-hand and walk you to a place where you are happy in your skin. Hopefully one day you will look around and see a place where your whole family is happy in its own skin.

24

School: January 2009

*"We must let go of the life we have planned,
so as to accept the one that is waiting for us."*

Joseph Campbell

My capacity for acceptance was pushed to the limit when we began looking at nurseries and schools for Sam. His fits were so bad and unpredictable a mainstream nursery couldn't cope with his needs, even with support. When Sam was three we visited two local special needs schools.

Stepping inside, I was submerged into a world where disability was an accepted norm. Previously, only at home was Sam normal and catered for like Jonah. Yet as I toured around, when I probably ought to have felt a sense of relief and belonging born out of being around people who understood and cared, the truth was I hated it. At the time, I wasn't prepared for it to be my world. I looked at all the other kids and couldn't get my head around Sam being part of their community. I struggled to come to terms with this being *our* community. After crying in the car parks, we decided on a school and began the task of getting Sam a statement of special educational needs.

It was long and arduous; much like the process of getting a wheelchair, or the right kind of care, or funding for Bobath, or anything else in this maze of a disabled world. Parents like me are required to spend hours of time and energy fighting to get anything done.

Sam's first day at school was the first milestone he reached alongside his peers. As I stood in our dining room contemplating the number of occasions I didn't think this day would come, I smiled at my little boy going to school. He had fought off infections, lived through near fatal seizures, and now he was sitting in his chair wearing his bright blue uniform, ready to embark on a whole new world without me. I swelled with gratitude at being able to witness this milestone and took a photo.

I remember being so proud of my own first day at school. Dad took a picture of me outside the back of our house before I left. There I stood by the gate to our backyard beaming from ear to ear with my pigtails and brown satchel. I was thrilled with my independence and excited at starting something new. Having just moved to Northern Ireland from Scotland everything was different.

As I looked at Sam, he hadn't developed any level of independence. I feared the changes he would not understand. I had spent the last three years with him as an extension of my own body. He was completely reliant on me like any newborn baby, and now I was to give him over to people who didn't know him, who wouldn't understand him, and couldn't possibly see him the way I did.

When my mum cared for Sam, I wrote out instructions for his daily routine. I detailed the medications required, the time he needed to be offered the toilet, his therapy and stretches, activities he may engage in, the music and TV he enjoyed, words he understood, when he was due his milk, how to handle his PEG tube, what to do if he started fitting, or vomited, or choked, or had a temperature. I gave a minute-by-minute account that covered three to four pages. Today Sam's 'passport' is over thirty-five pages long. When Jonah was looked after as a baby I made sure the babysitter knew when he ate and slept and that was it. Today he can express his own needs.

For the first term Sam went to the school nursery in the morning. I would collect him at lunchtime and be told he had a good day.

That was it.

'A good day.'

I had heard nearly every breath Sam had taken for the last three years and now all I was told was he'd had a good day. I really struggled with the lack of information. I knew I needed to let Sam go, to not be in control, but what could have been space in my day became a pressure. I had less time to fit in all the things therapists had told me were vital because I didn't know if they had been done. Thankfully the school was ready to hear my concerns and over time we developed a way of communicating with each other the information I felt was important.

For three years I collected Sam from school and it was a couple of years before I felt comfortable. When I saw the kids sitting waiting in the hall for transport home it felt so impersonal. I struggled imagining people looking at Sam in the same way I saw the other children. It wasn't that I didn't see their beauty or value, but I knew I wasn't seeing who they really were because amidst the noise and kerfuffle, the details were lost. I know when people see Sam they see a boy in a wheelchair who can't talk or do very much, yet I see so much more.

It has taken me years to embrace the beauty and chaos of Sam's school, appreciating the many staff who work continuously beyond the call of duty to give a full and vibrant experience of life to children like Sam.

During this process of acceptance and learning, we changed church. Our current church had seen us through the toughest time of our lives. They had sent us abroad and welcomed us home. Then they lived with us through our pregnancy, Sam's birth and early years. Leaving them was not an easy decision. It meant stepping away from friendships that had played a very important part in our lives.

Our decision to move was an attempt to make life resemble our values. It was the first recognisable step on a journey of making active choices; not just react to circumstances. We are passionate about touching people's lives with love. We want our faith to infuse our whole life. We imagined we would be living abroad but that was not the case. So when the opportunity arose, we threw ourselves into our local Baptist home mission church that focused on standing alongside the marginalised in our community and being church in new ways.

We continually tried to live the life we had expected, not the one we were living. We constantly used more energy than we had, and cracks started to form. Two things that bolstered me during this time were my friend Alex and a garden shed. Alex and I began meeting weekly and these debriefs became vital in allowing me time to reflect, relax and drink tea. The garden shed was actually a very simple but perfect summerhouse at the bottom of our small garden.

In the mornings, I slid out of bed while everyone else slept, headed downstairs and stumbled out of the back door holding a piping hot cup of tea. As I sat under a warm rug in my wooden haven, clasping my morning brew I was able to sigh. I had space, and just a few moments each day away from my responsibilities. Sometimes I listened to music, while at others I sat in silence and heard the street wake up.

Whether it was sunny or snowing, I snuck out to the summerhouse to find calm and freedom. For the rest of the day I would be at the beck and call of my family but for thirty minutes it was simply blankets, my thoughts, my Creator and me. I read my bible and prayed, asking for strength, hope and peace. In my solace, I began writing a diary as my cold fingers gripped a pen and scrawled letters across blank paper.

Mostly the pages spoke of my woes, as I tried to untangle my life and strived to gain perspective. As advent 2009 approached, my first diary entry declared my uncertainty of the year ahead. The last time we called an ambulance was only two weeks earlier. I didn't know how long Sam would live but I felt I needed to prepare for the worst.

As the tinsel and lights filled the windows of homes, I started thinking about Christmas. I believe in the story of a young woman who found herself in a mess; engaged to marry a man whilst carrying a baby that wasn't his. She embarked on a scary and rough ride. When Mary gave birth to Jesus she was homeless, destitute and starting a marriage on the most difficult of terms.

If I had been her, I would have felt abandoned by a God whom I had diligently served. Alone and scared, she must have felt forgotten and distant. Those around her may have thought these hard-luck times were her own doing and demonstrated God's disapproval. In my quiet summerhouse, I saw past the tinsel and tree, beyond the quaint, sterilised nativity and saw a frightened and lost young woman struggling to understand what was happening to her.

Without the saintly glow or iconic pale blue headscarf I

could relate to Mary, her sense of confusion and uncertainty. My life was no reflection of what I had hoped or expected. I couldn't see purpose, rhyme, or reason. Sam was living on the brink of death and our family edged perilously along the epilepsy tightrope. Then one morning I had a revelation. It didn't make any sense to Mary either.

Whether you think of the Christmas story as a fictional tale with a moral, or truth to be lived, the message is the same. At the centre of mess and confusion, something bigger, greater and more powerful can be happening. Mary couldn't possibly comprehend that in the midst of her difficulties something was taking place that would change the history of the world.

As I looked out of the picture window, towards my home I realised if I only saw goodness in the easy times then I might just be missing out on something truly great. Very often, the whys and hows of life cannot be explained. In my little summerhouse, tucked away from the world, I chose to try and continue down the road of acceptance to hope and freedom, even when it didn't make sense. There is a lot I don't understand but I live in hope that there is something, or someone greater participating in this messy world with me. I began to recognise that freedom arises from within my circumstances, rather than dependent on me escaping them.

When the Psalmist wrote, 'The Lord is my shepherd. I shall not want,' I decided that 'not wanting' was a choice of contentment. As I began to stop fighting the world in which I found myself, I was able to find more rest (sadly not in terms of sleep). It was only when I embraced my reality that I began finding my feet. I had to walk the path before me, not the one I had hoped for.

As my acceptance grew, so did my vision of myself. Since Sam had been born, I had worried what people thought when they saw me. I would catch my reflection as I walked with a child in a bright orange wheelchair and wondered how it had all happened and what must people be thinking? I had avoided Facebook and contacting old friends because I didn't want sympathy, or people's opinion of me warped.

As the fighting slowed, my muscles relaxed, acceptance grew and I began my rehab. Like an alcoholic in an AA meeting, I was able to stand up and say,

'My name is Rachel and my son is severely disabled.'

It was only when I realised that this fact didn't define me, that I was bigger than this detail of my life, could I bring it into conversation without awkwardness.

My journey of acceptance may never be complete. There are days of heartbreak when I appear to have done a complete u-turn and ended up a few miles back down the street. I look up to see buildings and markings on the road that indicate I am back where I was five years ago, or the day after Sam was born. The familiarity of the shop windows, packed with grief and regret are like old gloves – well-worn and easy to put on. Yet on these days I know the journey I have already taken, and covering old ground to get back to where I have come is swift.

As I talk with friends, I clearly see that although our roads are different, much of the difficult terrain and milestones are similar. It is comforting to notice the landmarks of their journey and acknowledge that I was once in that place and have moved further along the road. Sometimes it is only when I see myself reflected in my friends, or even the pages of this book, that I can see how far I have come.

25

Marathon

*"What has been will be again,
what has been done will be done again;
there is nothing new under the sun."*

Ecclesiastes 1v9

When Jonah was one I woke in an unfamiliar room with butterflies occupying my stomach. My friend Jo came in with a cup of tea, nervously whispering about breakfast. Like two kids preparing for a school trip, we crept around the flat getting everything ready. Once we'd eaten our porridge we hit the quiet streets of London and set off to catch a tube. At Victoria Station, a swathe of Flora London Marathon bags flocked towards the free trains to Blackheath and we squeezed on a carriage ready to depart.

At the start line, I stood amidst hundreds of people on their tiptoes, aching to begin. The atmosphere was at carnival pitch, with music blasting out of the temporary sound system. Putting on my running belt and attaching my energy gels helped me feel equipped for the task ahead. Having run a marathon a few years earlier, I knew I could go the distance.

I wished my life were as planned and predictable as the race I was facing. Without a route, distance or finish line I couldn't see how I should prepare myself for life as a mother. I didn't know what skills I might need or what lay ahead.

Amidst coffee mornings and physiotherapy, I struggled with a lack of sleep. Sam's poor seizure management resulted in him being agitated through the night and waking several times. We began having carers twice a week that stayed awake in Sam's room through the night.

I didn't enjoy going to bed knowing someone was wide-awake listening to my snoring but it was necessary. Sam's fits had become so unpredictable and life threatening that we sent an email to friends warning them that Sam was unstable, expectant that in the near future we may need to inform them he had died.

We began to take respite as a family at the local children's hospice, where nurses provided Sam's care. Over a twenty-four hour period, four to five nurses were required to give the care I gave every day. It was a relief when someone else was responsible for Sam, although I struggled when I felt they didn't do it correctly.

The food was great, the bed comfortable, and we had space in the day to relax and do fun things with Sam and Jonah. But guess what, I hated it.

Although I appreciated all the care, it was in a hospice.

hospice | ˈhɒspɪs| *noun*
a home providing care for the sick or terminally ill

The only place I could get enough support to provide a break for my family was where children go to die. The only reason we were eligible was because Sam had a life limiting condition; he isn't expected to grow up.

One evening we were sitting at dinner when an ambulance turned up with a couple and their newborn baby. The baby had only a few hours to live and the couple chose to walk around the gardens with their precious child, squeezing the essence out of every minute they had left.

171

As I sat finishing my meal, I looked across at Sam wondering how life would end for him. I looked at Jonah and thought about how I might explain his brother had died. In the weeks before we had begun making plans for what would happen in the event of Sam's death. I had met with the community palliative care nurse and discussed what would be the procedure if Sam had a fatal fit at home.

I looked out the window of the hospice and couldn't imagine the grief-stricken path that this young couple were embarking on, when my thoughts were interrupted by someone asking me if I wanted ice cream for pudding.

Death and ice cream.

At a hospice they live comfortably side-by-side and as much as the respite was a relief, the reality that Sam is not expected to live to adulthood was heartbreaking. I found it hard resting at the hospice and the frequent cancellations reduced the respite it provided. Life without respite, however, was long and arduous.

As I neared mile twenty of The London Marathon the running became painful and boring. I had been going for over three hours and I had more than an hour remaining. Each mile marker had a different backdrop but the expectation was the same: keep running.

My life felt like a marathon. I knew what was expected of me, but all I could see were the miles of road ahead and I was sick of running. I was tired of putting one foot in front of the other with aching muscles and my T-shirt rubbing.

I wanted a new phase, a new goal or a different task. The crises that came along didn't change. The season seemed limitless, as the guy who wrote Ecclesiastes pointed out centuries ago, 'There is nothing new under the sun.'

The truth was my struggles weren't new or different. My experience wasn't unique and many women I knew handled it with much more grace and gratitude. Yet when others hit the finish line of the struggle they faced, *my* life was stuck on mile twenty. It felt as though the pavement had been surreptitiously swapped for a treadmill with an unknown distance to run. My legs were frantically running but not covering any distance; our crises didn't stop, rather our challenges became normality.

When Sam got so heavy that I struggled carrying him upstairs we discussed with the council how to adapt our home but failed to meet a resolution. The arguing, alongside the sleepless nights, emergency trips to hospital and unremitting burden of care became too much. At the beginning of 2010 we put the house on the market and began looking for a bungalow.

Within six months and the usual house sale wrangling, moving day arrived. I went around our old home and took a video of each room. Our lives had been transformed in this place. We were very different people from the young couple who had moved in five years earlier.

It felt good to close the door and leave some memories behind. I needed to step away from a sense of loss and start a new phase. We drove up to our new home two miles along the Thames Estuary and waited to hear all the monies had exchanged hands. The call came and we stepped into our new house. Within two weeks all the adaptations had been made to make it our perfect home.

It was the small things that made the difference.

Suddenly we could sit around in our pyjamas eating breakfast together. Up until now, we all had to be dressed before going downstairs because Sam couldn't be carried back up. We also had more space to be hospitable. Our spare room soon housed Phil, a trainee minister placed in our church for a year.

Then a couple of months later our friend Hannah needed a place to stay and started sleeping on the living room floor: an agreement that lasted over six months. Our lives and home were full to overflowing.

A year later, the amount of care Sam required hadn't changed. As he grew so did his needs, and so did the gap between him and Jonah. Then reality hit; this was as good as it was going to get and life was still really hard work.

Jonah began school and there was even more space in my day but I still felt like I was drowning. Whether at home or away, Christmas, or a birthday, each day contained a never-ending to-do list. Just keeping Sam alive required twenty syringes of medicine to be drawn up daily, and he needed lifting more than a dozen times a day just for basic care. I couldn't just pop to the shops or decide to go somewhere on the spur of the moment because every outing required military precision and planning. What medicines should I take? How much milk will he need? Do we need to take specialist equipment? Will we need to stop en route for the toilet?

My day was so consumed with tasks, that there was rarely space to experience any physical or mental rest. Many interactions added to the strain, as conversations with blinkered professionals were exhausting and frustrating. For them my tidy house proved a good enough facade. I asked for help and explained my fatigue but it fell on deaf ears.

In the bag of goodies I received at the end of the marathon I was delighted to find a new running top with the word 'Finisher' blazoned across the middle. I decided that in order to finish the race I was running, I needed to complete the task on the little bit of pavement in front of me, only then would the next step become clear.

26

A Trip to the Library

"Your library is your paradise."

Desiderius Erasmus

To heighten my stress levels, Sam's frustration in communication resulted in him shouting a lot. Sam knows what he likes and more importantly he knows what he doesn't. He is a very emotional boy, who can scream and shout like someone has ripped his right arm off just because Jonah is watching the wrong TV programme.

This was stressful at home and unbearable when out. I was constantly worrying what people were thinking.

Take a trip to the library.

I imagine a trip to the library looking a lot like this...

I wander up the road pushing Sam as he smiles and mumbles, while I talk about our day and what we will do. Jonah saunters along next to us joining in the chit chat, excited about sharing books with his older brother.

When we arrive at the library I enter, grinning with pride, at the wealth of experiences I try to offer my delightful children. Quietly we settle down in a corner of the library. Sam sits attentive and eager to hear the first page of a book, while Jonah calmly flicks through the options. I sit on a chair next to Sam, holding his hand while I gently encourage Jonah to quickly make a choice.

Before long, Jonah is settled on my knee and I begin. Sam smiles with delight, while Jonah points at the pictures. The others in the library look on with respect and appreciation at how well I'm bringing up my children.

After a leisurely time of sharing books, we collect a wealth of material that barely touches our insatiable appetite for reading, and leave laden with books: happy and content.

In reality what actually happened...

I've been promising the boys all day that I will take them to the library but, with one thing and another, time flies until I realise I need to go now before it closes. As I prepare to leave, Sam indicates he needs the loo, so I lift him for the millionth time that day onto the bed and offer him the bottle, which he refuses. The grumbling and whining persists until I realise he wants to use the toilet 'properly', so I heave him on to the toilet seat and wheel him into the bathroom. Another ten minutes elapse as I'm running around the house trying to find all the overdue library books I keep getting automated voice messages about.

Finally, Sam has finished and I transfer him back onto the bed and get him dressed again before lifting him into his wheelchair. As I'm strapping Sam in, I notice Jonah hasn't got his shoes or coat on, even after the fifteen minute delay and me asking him a dozen times.

I start screaming instructions and he plays scared, running around the house not getting anything done. Eventually I give up and put Jonah's shoes on for him, while hissing through my teeth that he rarely listens to a word I say.

We rush out of the door fraught and flustered. Jonah runs off while I lock the gate and I'm left marching up the hill to the library after him. I reach the entrance sweating and wheezy. I rummage around in my handbag and take a quick puff of my inhaler. Bursting through the door we instantly shatter the calm and peace of the library atmosphere. Immediately, Sam arches back in his chair, turns his head and shouts at the top of his voice. I glance around hoping no one has noticed, only to see people promptly looking away, awkward and suddenly very busy with their books. I can't tell if they are disapproving, or worried about the noise, but as Jonah runs across the library to the kid's corner, I'm left whispering into Sam's ear.

Sam continues his protest and those who hear probably think he is a poor, frightful soul in pain or distress. Although his volume and intensity would indicate he has inadvertently had his left leg chopped off, what is actually happening is he's telling me he's angry. He loves going around in his wheelchair and he loves listening to stories, but he has absolutely no tolerance of the in-between time when he is neither being pushed nor reading a book.

I begin to ignore his shouting, much to the bewilderment of our fellow library visitors. They see an upset disabled little boy and I see a six-year-old having a tantrum. After a minute, I manage to locate Jonah who has found a book, a seat and made himself comfortable.

I begin to negotiate with Sam.

"Sam, stop shouting." The screaming ensues with real tears. "Listen, you can't talk to me while you are shouting." The sympathetic glances continue.

"Sam, do you want a book?" A pause.

"Sam, listen to me, would you like me to read you a story?"

"Mmm bu," Sam replies through tears. (Interpretation: "Yes please.")

"Ok, now wait a second and I'll find a book."

I ignore the screaming as it starts again, and frantically shuffle books trying to find one suitable.

"Jonah, are you going to join us?" No response.

"Jonah, listen to me. Do you want to read a story with Sam?"

"No, thanks. He's whining," comes the honest reply.

With no chairs available, I kneel on the floor next to Sam with his shouting and whaling echoing around the library.

"Here you go Sam, do you want me to read you this book?"

Instantaneously, Sam is silent and even the walls of the library sigh with relief.

"If you want me to read you a book you need to be quiet and say please."

"Mmm, buu."

"Ok. One day there lived..."

As I begin, I wipe the remnants of Sam's snotty tantrum from his face, trying not to let it interfere with the ebb and flow of my reading. When the last page of the book approaches, Sam notices the change in my tone of voice and begins a full throttle moan. After only one book I feel watched and wrung out. With the speed of lightning, I offer to put his music on so he can hear it from the headrest on his wheelchair. Immediately he concurs.

I stagger up from kneeling on the floor feeling much older than my years. I tentatively approach Jonah and for a couple of short minutes we share a book before more thundering groans emanate from Sam.

Exhausted, I grab the first ten books I find and try to usher Jonah out of the library. He begins to argue, complaining we haven't been there long enough and these aren't the books he wanted. After a fully-fledged western showdown, I marginally win the duel of authority with my four-year-old before limping out of the library wounded and beleaguered.

We walk home and, rather than appreciating the warming sun or flowers we pass, I dream of being home within my own four walls void of stares and expectations. I unlock the back door and glance up at the clock, only thirty minutes has passed since I left and yet I feel as though I have run 10k.

I flick on the kettle for a much needed cup of tea and Sam begins to complain.

"Sorry Sam, I'm making a cup of tea. I know it's loud and is interfering with you listening to your music but you aren't the only person living in this house."

27

Travelling Without Baggage

"It is during our darkest moments that we must focus to see the light."

Aristotle Onassis

When we realised everything beyond the island we lived on was out of bounds, we decided that Tim and I would take it in turns to go abroad, alone. Travelling was still something we loved and it renewed us.

Tim went first. He flew to the Philippines and spent eight days with his brother, Chris, who was living there at the time. At home I dealt with nits, had my birthday and juggled my boys without dropping them - a true mark of success. When it was my turn my friend Nora and I flew to Prague for a girly road trip. We hired a car and I drove us to Vienna and back.

Nora lives in Scotland and we rarely get to see each other, but having lived together before Tim and I married, we knew each other pretty well. In between us arguing about the things we normally disagree on, we had a fantastic time exploring, eating and resting. The days were long and time dragged, but in a really good way.

A few days into our trip, we took a leisurely walk across Charles Bridge. We listened to a band of men entertaining passersby with traditional music, painting each face with a smile and causing many to stop and savour the moment. Then, while Nora was off looking at something creative, I rested in the courtyard of Prague Castle. Sitting on the cobbled street, I saw castle guards stride past, important and busy; dressed in their pristine pale blue uniforms, with guns resting sprightly on their right shoulder. I could see tourists taking photos and arguing over maps in various languages, while children ran along the cobbled streets playing games.

It was a warm day, making my jacket redundant on the stone ground. I leaned against the towering walls of the surrounding buildings, sipped water and smiled, thankful for the whole experience. I was grateful for how long the hours had become, how my day was no longer segregated into sections of time, each related to administering medications, feeding or toileting.

When I woke up in the morning, I only had myself to think about. I was shocked that I rarely gave home a moments thought. This foreign place was unreal and distant, filling my head with dreams of what could have been, while home was a parallel universe. I felt relaxed and as though I was being me for the first time in years.

The way I was living was such a contrast to my real life that I couldn't understand how they could co-exist on the same planet. As a wife and mother there were days when I felt my only purpose was to look after everyone else. I couldn't see myself in the mass of everyone else's needs. I had become a blur. I was weary with a tiredness that makes your bones ache and is untouched by a good night's sleep.

I wanted to enjoy loving and caring for my sons without the burden of disability. I was sick of new trials and wanted rest. My thoughts cascaded forward and rose around me like the towering castle walls.

Sitting alone in the shadows, feeling trapped and hemmed in, my heart raced and I called Tim. The ring tone echoed in my ear until I heard a voice.

"Hello."

"Hi, its me."

"Hi, how are you? What are you doing?"

"I'm just sitting outside Prague Castle. Nora is off somewhere and it's a lovely warm day."

"That sounds pretty good."

"It is…" I choked as tears began to trip my cheeks. "But I don't want to come home." The tone of my voice and sincerity of words meant Tim didn't hesitate taking me seriously.

This wasn't about having a lovely holiday and wishing it didn't end. I no longer wanted to deal with what I had left behind. I wanted to do a Thelma and Louise, without the cliff bit at the end. I couldn't face returning to my life.

I explained to Tim that I couldn't keep doing all that was expected of me. It was too much and too hard. Understandably, he was heartbroken and because he is a truly remarkable man, he stopped what he was doing, sat at the end of the phone and allowed me to weep and share my fears and feelings. I tried to help him understand emotions that I barely understood myself.

To say I love Tim and the boys doesn't express the depth and breadth of admiration and devotion I feel. They are my world and make me whole. I enjoy life and loving my boys. Yet, as I sat on those stones over eight hundred miles from home I had glimpsed another life. It was an easier life with freedom, space, spontaneity and a lot more sleep. I tasted what I had known before and missed so desperately. I knew I had changed forever and there was no going back but part of me wanted to run away and not return. Home felt like a straitjacket. I realised a lot of it stemmed from the expectations of perfection and productivity I placed on myself, but I didn't know how else to exist.

It was as though someone had removed from my eyes a pair of heavy sunglasses. I had been walking around a dimly lit world, appreciating and enjoying everything but oblivious to its true colours. I had failed to see a bright world with sunlight streaming into my eyes, painting vivid pictures on my retina.

In that moment, I wallowed in believing I had been right the night after Sam was born. It was harder him living.

"I just don't know if I can handle the busyness of caring for the boys." I confessed.

"I can understand that. It's really hard work and you do a great job."

"I feel so squeezed and each day I'm less and less like me."

"We need to make changes. We need to give you more space and time. It's hard Rachel. It's really hard."

As Tim spoke and soothed me, I sobbed with guilt and fear. I didn't love my children any less than any other mother but life felt so incredibly hard, that I dared to imagine life without them and for a moment it seemed like a better option.

Thankfully, I didn't spend long in that place. Soon my love swamped my sense of loss. Tim and I spoke for about twenty minutes and by the end of the conversation, I was more coherent and capable of seeing more of the beauty in my family, hopeful that life could be more sustainable.

That evening I called again to reassure Tim that I would come home.

Once in Southend, I slipped back into the chaotic

routine of duties and responsibilities but something had changed inside me. I wanted a life that was both sustainable and enjoyable. My family is the most important thing to me and I needed to value the time we had together. It could all dramatically change at any time. I would never again experience Sam being six or Jonah being four. It only happens once before it becomes a memory.

Since this trip, Tim still lets me go away but each time I'm about to step out the door, I look back as he says, "You will come back won't you?"

Inevitably, I respond with a smile and a kiss.

"Of course I will. I love you." As I walk out the door, my to-do list is screwed up. Yet as I leave home, the biggest part of me stays behind.

28

Working and Weeping

"When Moses' hands grew tired, they took a stone and put it under him and he sat on it. Aaron and Hur held his hands up---one on one side, one on the other---so that his hands remained steady"

Exodus 17v12

I knew things needed to change but, like facing the chaotic scene of a filled nappy that has breached its walls, I didn't know where to start. The stress of Sam's shouting, both at home and outside caused a strain that can't be quantified. One minute he can be his usual happy self, smiling his infectious smile, and then suddenly the shouting begins. A pleasant time as a family or journey in the car could be hijacked by screaming demands. With his limited communication, there were times when we simply didn't know, or couldn't give him what he wanted, leaving us listening to incessant screaming and shouting.

Then there have been times when the planning and preparation has paid off. When we chose to go for a walk in the countryside, pulled on our wellies, timed the toileting and feeding, and headed off. The sun streaked through the winter sky and Sam's Hippocampe wheels got laden with mud, as we enjoyed being together as a family. Jonah would chatter, while Sam 'cooed' and 'aahed', raising his left hand for someone to hold. Or, there were the times we sat together in the living room all snug under a duvet watching a film, or in the hospice swimming pool, where we enjoyed quality family time.

These times happened because we made them happen, soaking up every drop. Our boys are a delight and I'm my family's biggest fan. However, everything takes a lot of energy. Making holidays and weekends more than just existing has been hard work and therefore, they are often absent of rest. Unsurprisingly, the fatigue was joined by more emotional meltdowns.

One day I was trying to buy an outfit for the boys to wear at a family wedding. With Jonah I cooed at what would make him look cute and smart, all grown up and handsome. With Sam I didn't have that luxury. Firstly, I needed to consider the practicalities of what I could get on him, then what would be comfortable sitting in his chair and whether it could be adapted.

As I stood in the aisle holding on to a shirt sleeve, I stared into the middle distance and my mind wandered. I began recalling my normal and uncomplicated pregnancy. I remembered Sam's twenty-week scan. We chose not to know the sex of our baby and so chatted merrily, while the ultrasound scanner smeared the slimy gel over my belly with the screen pointed away. I recalled the strange feeling, as I held the fuzzy black and white photo of the shadows that depicted my baby's limbs and features; our baby was growing and healthy.

Then the reality of the present hit and I riled at how far I had come from uncomplicated joy, to the perplexing task of buying my son an outfit.

I began weeping.

Embarrassed, I looked around and made for the exit. I hurried out of the shop and straight to my car without any purchases. Once safely inside the relative soundproofing of my wheelchair adapted vehicle, I wailed. Noise and snot joined my tears, as I rested my head on the steering wheel and allowed my body to shake and heave. For me, it seems the passing years haven't dampened the grief of these times, as the 'wave' crashes over me once more. Sometimes it's just a windy day and high-tide kind of wave, which sprays the concrete promenade with water containing the same salty tang of my tears.

On this particular day, a ripple of memories catalysed emotions that replicated a tsunami and I was battered and washed off course. Once I had wiped away my tears, I drove home and gathered myself ready to collect Jonah from school and begin the 'afternoon shift'.

A day later I lay on the sofa with a heavy heart, as I nestled under a woollen throw to watch some trash TV. These emotional meltdowns have continued, but now I ride them out rather than fighting them. I trust that tomorrow will be a better day and give myself the grace to recover from the battering.

Through it all Tim continued to work full time as a GP, before coming home and being an incredible husband and father. Putting down his workbag each day, he would immediately begin helping me with the boys. He diligently carried the burden of being the rock of the family and supporting me as I tried to make life more sustainable.

When the cracks started showing in Tim, it took us both by surprise. He began feeling anxious and stressed in situations he previously found easy. The significant decisions he made every day at work became palpable and overbearing. He had been storing up years of physical and emotional stress, locking it away like most 'good' men, until he couldn't hold back the tide any more.

As a result, he took a short time off work and started the long process of facing the past. It was seven years before we saw the benefit of counselling but there Tim found he had a well of tears swollen from years of neglect.

A wonderful young man once came to stay at our home. He wasn't with us long before he asked what was wrong with Sam. He excitedly explained that his older sister also had cerebral palsy. Within minutes, we had established she was very similar to Sam but about twenty years older. At the time, we were carrying out the boys' bedtime routine; Tim and I went into the bathroom and simply looked at each other aghast. After the kids were in bed, we had a long chat with our new friend and he shared how his family was completely normal to him. He had never known anything else but found it difficult watching his parents struggle.

In bed that night, Tim and I stayed awake talking. The feelings of our conversation were raw, painful and felt entirely unnatural. We found ourselves dreading the prospect of struggling with the same issues, writing the same grumpy letters to the council, weeping the same tears and constantly striving and fighting for just about everything for another twenty years. This conversation heightened an already on-going discussion about how we make our life more sustainable; how we make the pattern of our living capable of lasting the long haul.

We both realised so many things we thought were important or 'expected' of us needed to go. Together we took time out. We stripped our lives bare and began the process of rebuilding them based on what we had, could and wanted to do. We needed to live within our reality. It meant releasing friendships that were draining, and cutting back on responsibilities.

The first thing to go was 'busyness' as a status symbol.

We no longer strived to be successful or productive but

rather live a life that was abundant and sustainable. Tim needed to do more than work and care for his family. I needed to live beyond the world of disability. We needed to find ways to rest and have fun. I had to stop feeling guilty for sitting down while Tim was at work. I took up knitting, occasionally watched quality programs such as *The OC* and my much-loved chick flicks. I even dared to put on my trainers once in a while and not just to put out the rubbish.

We decided it was important to claw back a Sabbath. I felt I hadn't had a consistent day off for years. All that I needed to do for Sam every day felt like work, partly because I was so wrung out. Like an RNLI lifeboat, my mum and dad came to the rescue and began having Sam after school and overnight every week. Tim tried to have time off on the same day and routine space to rest and rejuvenate was born.

We created quality time with each other; going for a walk, or just sitting in front of the fire to watch a film before sneaking in an afternoon nap. We had space to be us. Then after school, Jonah joined in the fun when we could head out for a meal, run around the park or wander down to the amusements and waste some money.

We also made the tough decision to have holidays without Sam. Each year we tried to have a weekend away, just Tim and I, and then a break with Jonah. These trips provided us with a level of rest and recuperation not possible with Sam, although I spend the whole time feeling my right arm is missing.

The difficult choices continued as we began paying for more night-carers, recognising that the lack of sleep was killing our spirits and shrinking our lives. The reality of not being able to do it on our own was tough. For me I had to quiet the screaming in my head suggesting I was a rubbish mum for needing others to care for my son.

Finally, I allowed myself to believe this was how we were created. For so long I had thought abundance and prosperity were about independence and productivity. It was a revelation when I began to see success and abundance as interdependence and community: sharing, loving and rest. I needed to be helped by others both physically and emotionally. If I couldn't take help without feeling judged, then I couldn't give it without judging. All the expectations I thought people were placing on me, were in fact my own.

A year after leaving my job as a diabetes practice nurse I went back to the surgery and they kindly gave me a few hours' work a week. It was good to have something outside our home and disability to think about. I also started giving myself time every week to write and reflect. Words started pouring out of me as I visited the shadows of my story. Shining a light on all that had happened breathed fresh air into my past.

Most importantly we committed ourselves more passionately to sharing our journey and lives with friends who could rejoice and mourn with us. We sacrificed activities and duties, to create the time and energy for living alongside people who could hold up our hands when we became tired, because we all get tired.

29

Funerals: 18th October 2012

"Behold I will create new heavens and a new earth.
The former things will not be remembered...
but be glad and rejoice forever in what I will create..."

Isaiah 65v17-18

In a large cavernous building I joined my local disabled community. The icons and echoes, order and protocols encased us as we sat shoulder to shoulder. We are a mixed bunch of people: professionals, parents and friends from all walks of life. We gathered in our pink and orange uniforms and sat with our breaths forming a mist in the cold air. As I looked around, I saw familiar faces from various corners of this unique, intimate world. Our sense of community and belonging warmed us as we sat to celebrate the life and mourn the death of my friend's thirteen year old son, Aidan.

He had cerebral palsy, like Sam, and blessed his family with a similar level of smiles and laughter. He was surrounded with love and one unassuming day he was found in bed having died peacefully and silently in the night. It was sudden, unexpected and shocking, yet a potential reality for families like ours. No amount of logical discussion had prepared me for the level of grief and loss present in the church.

The day before, my parents had attended the funeral of a

young man from the youth group of their last church. He had a thriving career, devoted girlfriend, loving family and future of dreams yet unrealised. Before he started his career as a solicitor, he took a trip to Mount Everest. Tragically, his plane crashed and he was one of seven Britons that made up the nineteen strong death toll. Unsurprisingly, the talk of his family, friends and colleagues were of a wasted life, his loss of career, marriage and future. All that he was destined to achieve never came to pass and with a great sense of loss all who loved and knew him were left with memories of the past and dreams of what might have been.

Aidan's funeral was different. The sense of loss was just as great, but it wasn't related to potential or future, it was simply the loss of joy in the presence of an amazing young man; not because of what he had achieved, or may achieve, but just because of who he was. In essence, we mourned the loss of Aidan's spirit and personality. We mourned the joy, love and huge smile that created the simple, pure and vulnerable relationships saved exclusively for kids like him and Sam.

There are days when it feels too much, too sad, too tiring and too heartbreaking to care for Sam but loving him is always better than the alternative. The heaviness of caring for Sam is a very separate experience from the joy of being his mum. The relationship created by him and me is greater than our two parts. My love for Sam and our relationship is the purest I have. It is not weighed or balanced with potential gain or expectations of future rewards.

In logical terms, Sam's life isn't financially viable. He will never practically contribute to his community in a meaningful, productive way. Put simply, he is a burden on society and us. It is harsh, brutal and true that if we apply the most commonly used measures of value, Sam is of little worth and his life of little value. Yet when we apply measures of productivity, intellect and contribution we miss the essence of life.

Sam brings something unique to every relationship and he adds a quality to every gathering of people. That is because relationship isn't logical. Having babies or getting married isn't logical. Love, God, faith, forgiveness and the spiritual world aren't logical.

I have been known to occasionally watch daytime TV such as *Cash in the Attic* or *Flog It!*, while Tim is more highbrow and saves himself for the Antiques Road Show. These programmes examine items, look at their intricate detail or public appeal, and place a price on them. The fun of the auction programmes is that you then get to actually see what they are worth. They are sold to the highest bidder and what was an educated prediction becomes a reality. Sometimes people are disappointed as well-loved family heirlooms are sold cheaply with a brusque disregard for the memories they contain. On other days, a couple of people in the auction room want Lot number 228 and as a result it soars in cost, surprising the professionals and sellers alike.

As the auction room demonstrates, worth isn't just measured in terms of the intrinsic value of an object. It comes from us; how much we think it is worth, how much we treasure it.

Sam's body is no masterpiece. His limp limbs hang from his body without purpose or strength. His body could be considered broken and void of purpose, yet a chewed Biro used to sign The Beatles record deal could fetch thousands of pounds because people value the story and what it signifies. Equally, my son and his body become increasingly valuable and treasured, as

193

those that love and care for him recognise the spirit, person and story he holds.

A piece of artwork put together by children at the hospice was unveiled in 2012. We went along to its presentation, as pieces Sam and Jonah created were part of the sculpture. It used a Helen Keller quote as its central message:

'The best and most beautiful things in the world cannot be seen or even touched – they must be felt with the heart.'

All the wondrous, mystical and greatest parts of our lives don't fit into logic and can't be explained by theory. They are felt and lived, experienced beyond our five senses. They may not be pinned down or articulated, but they are no less real or life-sustaining then oxygen. The love of a spouse or child may be expressed, but rarely adequately explained, because it is spiritual and mystical, not tangible and defined.

When I no longer have Sam, I won't grieve for what he could have been or what he failed to realise. I have been grieving those things since the day he was born. When I no longer have Sam, I will grieve that I no longer have Sam. I will miss him and I will miss our relationship. In the deepest way, I will ache at no longer living with his spirit and character in my life and my home. I will miss the atmosphere and presence he creates by simply being him.

In May 2012 my wonderful ninety-seven year old grandma died. She was an incredible, gentle, inspiring lady with a big heart and strong faith. In dying terms, her death was as good as it gets. Within a few short days, she slowly gave up and her family spent some beautiful times with her before she died. We sang her favourite hymns, held her hand, and told her how wonderful and loved she was. The loss she was to our family heightens my awareness of the harrowing experience losing Sam will be.

Grandma's death was timely. It was what was best for her. She had lived a long and love-filled life. When Sam no longer fills my days with his demands, and our family is left with a Sam-shaped hole, the chasm will be catastrophic. But this is my truth - my reality. It may be in months or years and any number of terrible or wonderful things may happen along the way. Because Sam and his disabilities consume so much of my life, when he is no longer with us, I will need to relearn to live again, in the way I did the day he was born.

At Aidan's funeral we sang *All Things Bright and Beautiful* as the unfairly small bright blue coffin was carried in. When it came level with our row, our voices dried up and silence fell. Our words hushed with the reality of grief and tragedy. We were encouraged by the priest to celebrate Aidan's life and have confidence that he was in heaven, doing cartwheels. The grief of parents, brothers and close friends was so brutal, yet as I sat on my hard pew I knew I had already had a glimpse of heaven in Aidan. Heaven isn't just an experience saved for when we've died; we have the power to bring heaven on earth. The love and joy of Sam and Aidan are a touch of heaven here and now.

The truth is no one knows the future, but I expect to plan a funeral for Sam in a way that I don't anticipate with Jonah. As I looked around the church, I saw half a dozen mums whose tears stung with the knowledge of 'this could be me'. This truth, this reality, has made me want to be more present in today.

30

Another View

*"We are not necessarily doubting that God will do the best for us;
we are wondering how painful the best will turn out to be."*

C.S. Lewis

When Sam got home from school the day after the funeral, I did all his essential jobs quickly so I could just sit down and hold him. The next morning I woke at five o'clock having not been woken through the night, something that hadn't happened for months. I held my breath as I waited to hear him on the baby monitor. After a few long seconds he sighed and so did I. When he woke, I climbed out of bed and into his.

I wanted to soak up precious time with my boy and within thirty minutes, Jonah came into the room. By six-thirty, the three of us were reading the book *The Fourth King*. It's about a king trying to join the three wise men, seeking a meeting with baby Jesus. Unfortunately, he is waylaid saving children, helping strangers, and even helping Mary and Joseph escape with their newborn to Egypt. It is a story that highlights the importance of the journey, rather than the destination, and the funeral had reminded me that relationships mean more than achievements.

The pain and joy that tomorrow might bring can daunt me, so I treasure the gift of today. I live with faith, and trust that no matter what, if I look, there is the possibility of love and peace. Hindsight has taught me that my life smells most strongly of my Creator when it is at its toughest and messiest, although that knowledge doesn't make the experience any less painful. I have found that in the middle of a dark wilderness, the light is most potent and colour most vibrant.

The story I am living seems a million miles from the one I anticipated. My life often feels held in the shadow-lands of another world, unknown to many. I walk a journey and road most people are sheltered from and oblivious to. I have tried to live with my faith supporting me but, at times, it has provided more questions than answers and I have experienced more anger than comfort.

There have been days when life was simply more than I could bear, when cries of help to my Creator appeared to be left unanswered. I think we all travel through life carrying an emotional backpack. Some people don't notice the drain of this luggage, while others try to look the other way.

Often we assume we understand the contents of each other's rucksack and are tempted to compete for the title of most laden, but there is no competition. There is only value in sharing the contents of our load, as we journey together and shoulder the weight of each other's burdens.

On my own journey the weight of my backpack changes. Some days it contains the pain of missed dreams and never hearing my son say 'Mum.' When I go to the park it is loaded down with the disappointment of my son not enjoying the slide. During games with nieces and nephews, it digs into my shoulders and throbs with the ache of fantasies of what could have been. On days out, I'm crippled by places that are inaccessible and facilities that are inadequate. Every day my rucksack is plagued with fatigue. However, I love my beautiful boy with a capacity that I could not understand without him. The joy his smile and giggles bring, along with the love he creates around him, is extraordinary. I am his biggest fan, loudest advocate and a very proud mum.

As I have stopped and reflected on my memories, with all their inaccuracies and distortions, I clearly see my life as a collage of experiences. Some appeared mundane or normal, yet turned out to be distinctly less common. Often life drifted past, quietly forming and shaping me.

Then my defining moment came and my life will always be described as before or after. Sam's birth pivots the two halves of my life story so far. His arrival catapulted me into another world. His life and disabilities intertwined with my own to create a new language, scenery and culture that has transformed me. Nothing has smelt, tasted, looked or felt the same ever again, and as a result I think and live differently. Yet as the climate of my world changes, I am learning to love the skies I'm under.

From the collage of my memories, I have tried to piece together a vision of my present. Like creating a mosaic from shattered tiles, my life is made up of broken pieces fashioned together into something priceless and more beautiful.

I seek to rest in a joy that is not tainted or dented by circumstances. I seek a peace that is beyond logic or understanding. I yearn to love without fear and live a life with the exuberance, authenticity, simplicity, vulnerability and joy that I most clearly and beautifully see in my son, Sam.

Epilogue
December 2014

"Life isn't about waiting for the storm to pass.
It's about learning to dance in the rain"

Vivien Greene

People have all sorts of spiritual guides, and mine include Pixar and Disney. I was gripped by *The Croods* message of daring to follow the sun into a better tomorrow before Elsa came along and implored me to 'Let it Go...' She assured me that 'with some distance everything seems small and the things that once controlled us can't get to us at all.' So I'm trying to live in the truth of her words; allowing time and distance to give perspective and truth.

I love a good chick-lit book with a happy ending, passionate embrace and idyllic sunset. Yet my life doesn't have a Disney ending, because each sunset is followed by the sunrise of a new day. It may be an uneventful day of mundane happenings, or it might become one of my defining moments. As days turn to weeks, my life can feel stagnant and unchanging, yet nothing really stays the same. Either a situation changes or I am changed by it. Usually there is an intricate dance between the two that results in a new creation.

It seems I am not a super-woman, neither am I Lara Croft, Florence Nightingale or Mary Poppins. I write my kids' names in their school uniforms rather than sew them and my husband bakes more than me. Each day I try to accept who I am, along with my frailties, adapting to my emotions rather than striving to change them. I'm ready to be transformed by every situation I find myself in, although I reserve the right to have a two-year-old hissy-fit tantrum in the process.

Today, I accept that striving for balance means saying no and getting help. Weekly I fluctuate between enjoying the space to write, read or rest, and struggling against surging feelings of guilt. I'm still learning to allow my faith's heart for community and interdependence to drown out my own Western attitude of solitude and self-sufficiency.

Time has taught me that dealing with a diagnosis is not the same as handling the daily busyness it brings. A diagnosis becomes normality but as its backpack rests discreetly on my shoulders, I can still be overwhelmed. I have adapted to my life, although it is tiring, and at times relentless. I carry on travelling with the support of family and friends who step in when I don't have the energy to stand on my own.

Today, Sam is stable, beautiful and fun. Some weeks are tough but sleep helps, as do good friends and chocolate. When the nights are long, so are the days but Sam makes me smile every day and occasionally makes me weep. Jonah is independent, thoughtful and shows us a capacity for loving and acceptance that is inspiring. Most importantly, I travel this road with my greatest friend and wonderful husband, sharing the views, tears and joy.

Most days my thoughts of the future remain silently embedded at the back of my mind. I try to spend more time in today and grow daily in my admiration for the many women around me who care for their children, silently, diligently and patiently.

Is this life what I hoped or expected? No.

Do I wish it had turned out differently? Yes.

Do I regret it? No.

Is it hard? Yes, but hard isn't the same as bad. The pleasure of running a marathon only occurs because of the sweat in getting to the end. The dazzle of gold is brighter in the sifting pan than on the jeweller's shelf.

This isn't a typical happy ending, nor is it a tragedy. It's quite simply living life in hope. Tim and I have dared to hope again and as I write this I am five months pregnant. We dared to dream, to live and love beyond today. Who knows where this path will take us, but today we are exercising the art of taking another breath and choosing courage amidst our fears.

When you read the last page of this book, you will choose to read another and more pages will be turned. Tonight we will sleep and our minds will be filled with dreams and within them our sons may walk and talk. Then in the morning, we will wake to our reality and there beauty can be found.

Glossary

Cerebral Palsy Impaired muscle coordination and movement with or without other disabilities, normally caused by damage to the brain or nervous system.

Continuous Positive Airway Pressure (CPAP) A machine that uses air pressure to keep the airways open.

Clonazepam, diazepam and lorazepam Sedating medications that can be used to stop fitting.

EEG Electroencephalogram is a recording of brain activity obtained by attaching small sensors to the scalp. These sensors then record the electrical impulses produced by the brain.

GOSH Great Ormond Street Hospital

Hippocampe An all-terrain wheelchair that gives the freedom to go previously inaccessible places.
(http://www.hippocampe.co.uk)

Hypoxic Ischaemic Encephalopathy The term used for injuries in a baby caused by low oxygen. A lack of oxygen frequently damages the brain and other organs.

Intraosseous The insertion of a needle into the bone of the lower leg to inject fluids or drugs directly into the marrow.

MRI scan Or magnetic resonance imaging scan, is a painless scan used to take detailed images of the body.

Mzungu A word commonly used in Uganda to mean white person.

Nasogastric tube A narrow flexible tube passed via the nose into the stomach and is used for feeding.

Neonatal Care The care for newborn infants, up to 28 days after birth. The term neonatal comes from neo, 'new', and natal, 'pertaining to birth or origin'.

Neurologist A doctor specialising in diseases of the nervous system.

Opthalmologist A doctor specialising in conditions of the eye.

Palliative Care The care of the terminally ill, or children with life-threatening or life-limiting conditions.

PEG A percutaneous endoscopic gastrostomy (PEG) tube is a flexible tube inserted through the abdomen into the stomach. It allows fluids and medications to be put directly into the stomach without needing to be eaten or swallowed.

PH strip A small strip of coloured paper that turns red when in contact with acidic gastric juices. Used to indicate the correct position of a nasogastric tube in the stomach.

Physiotherapy The treatment of a condition using methods such as massage, heat and exercise.

Red book The personal child health book given to parents/carers at a child's birth.

Rescue Medication is the term used for drugs that are given to stop a seizure.

Special Care Baby Unit or Neonatal Unit A hospital ward for babies in the neonatal stage. Neonatal intensive care is for the most seriously ill babies.

Tasters are small amounts of food given to try and help a child enjoy or experience a food or flavour.

Ventilation When a machine mechanically moves air into and out of the lungs, providing the mechanism of breathing for a patient who can't breathe, or is breathing insufficiently.

Acknowledgements

This book started with me tapping away on my iPad in our summerhouse in 2012. It only got this far with thanks to:

Tim, who has been by my side at every step; thank you for enabling me to escape and write, and for being my most helpful critic, biggest fan and best friend.

My mum and dad, who have loved, encouraged, wept, celebrated and supported me. I can't thank you enough.

Alex and Kezia, who listened, talked, read and re-read my musings, encouraging me along the way.

David and Janine for your love and support.

Our wonderful community; especially the Hooks', Wrights, Hunts, Englands, Duprees, Haswells, Crabbs, Osler-Meades, Coles, Domineys, Durrants, Bex, Hannah, WBC, CFS, New Horizons, Valkyrie and Kingsdown.

The charities and organisations who support us; Little Havens Hospice, Together for Shorter Lives, EPIC, Southend Sunflower Trust, Scope, Newlife Foundation, Wipe Away Those Tears, Make a Wish, The Music Man Project, Southend Toy Library and the Bobath Centre.

Doreen, who is simply wonderful in every way.

My new writing friends, Debbie, Viv, Rowena and Judith.

Sue Atkinson at TLC, Claire, Ivan and www.franhallwriting.com; who didn't laugh at my mistakes.

The staff at 4edge and Hutchinscreative.

And especially the other mums who walk this path alongside me.

Finally, my beautiful boys, Sam, Jonah and Ethan; there's nothing that makes me more proud than being your mum.

About the Author

 Rachel lives in Southend-on-sea with her husband, Tim, and their three sons, Sam, Jonah and Ethan. She passes time by loving wonderful boys, doing laundry, picking up Lego (and other items) off the floor, having tea with her mum and Doreen, writing, and occasionally working as a diabetes practice nurse.

She loves hearing people's stories and encouraging others with her own family's story; either by talking to individuals, large groups, or through her blog. If you want to share your own story, or book Rachel to speak at your event she can be contacted via her website: www.bornattherighttime.co.uk or by email: bornatthewrighttime@gmail.com